A DEVOTIONAL JOURNEY
through

PROVERBS

31 REFLECTIONS
and INSIGHTS

Anna Haggard

GENERAL EDITOR

Our Daily Bread
Publishing™

A Devotional Journey through Proverbs:
31 Reflections and Insights from Our Daily Bread
© 2021 by Our Daily Bread Ministries

Illustrations by Veris Studio
Interior design by Kris Nelson/StoryLook Design

Library of Congress Cataloging-in-Publication Data

Title: A devotional journey through Proverbs : 31 reflections and insights
  from Our daily bread.
Other titles: Our daily bread.
Description: Grand Rapids : Our Daily Bread Ministries, [2021] | Summary:
  "A Devotional Journey through Proverbs walks you through a chapter of
  Proverbs each day. With the full Bible text, a devotional reading,
  additional insights and word studies, beautiful color illustrations, and
  space to journal, you can reflect on and respond to each passage in your
  own way and grow in the wisdom of God"-- Provided by publisher.
Identifiers: LCCN 2020044611 | ISBN 9781640700833 (paperback)
Subjects: LCSH: Bible. Proverbs--Devotional literature.
Classification: LCC BS1465.54 .D48 2021 | DDC 242/.5--dc23
LC record available at https://lccn.loc.gov/2020044611

Printed in the United States of America
21 22 23 24 25 26 27 28 / 8 7 6 5 4 3 2 1

*The fear of
the LORD
is the
beginning
of wisdom.*

PROVERBS 9:10

Proverbs

Embracing God's Wisdom in the Book of Proverbs

Over a year ago, I decided to change my life. I told only my husband about my intentions because I wasn't completely sure whether I would follow through. Would I really make the necessary choices to embrace change? I wanted to do the work quietly and without the pressure of others knowing.

With God's help, I did; I've been able to stick to a plan of healthy eating. Losing weight shows on the outside, but the deep work inside is also meaningful. Meal by meal and day by day, leaning on God, I've been able to persevere, paying attention to my motivations and the needs of my body. I can see now how the fruits of building resilience and exercising self-control can manifest themselves in other areas of my life too.

Embracing wisdom is a bit like the dilemma of what to eat today. People won't necessarily see our moment-by-moment decisions to live according to God's principles, but they will glimpse our character transformed. They'll be able to witness the work of the Spirit as we become more loving, kind, peaceful, wise, self-controlled, giving, and gracious. These changes may show up in everyday moments—like putting someone else's needs before our own or holding our tongue when we're irritated or exhausted. Or they could influence the direction of our lives—such as exhibiting the courage to take a different job, to learn a new skill, to stand against injustice. The possibilities are as unique and individual as we each are.

Where can we find this wisdom? Direction on how to live wisely—in tune with the leading of the Spirit in day-to-day life—can be found throughout the Bible, but a good place to start if you long to grow in wisdom is the book of Proverbs. Packed with pithy sayings, this book is not one that we'll probably read long passages from, but we can savor its words of wisdom and advice. Through applying its guidance, we can grow to be more like Jesus.

Proverbs is part of the Bible's Wisdom Literature, the Old Testament genre focused on wise living. King Solomon is the primary person connected to this genre, with wisdom being his life's pursuit. When God asked what he could grant Solomon, the king asked for "a discerning heart" (1 Kings 3:9). And God responded graciously, making Solomon the wisest man (v. 12). With his legacy of wisdom, Solomon is considered the main contributor of Proverbs, his work inspired by God.

This Old Testament book can be broken up into three sections. The first, chapters 1 through 9, includes lectures to a young person, "my son" (1:8), and centers on the fear of the Lord—with *fear* meaning a holy awe and reverence. Then the bulk of the book, chapters 10 through 29, includes the short sayings most associated with Proverbs. These word pictures compare or contrast everyday things in order to reveal truth. The last two chapters of Proverbs form the conclusion, with Proverbs 31 providing an inspiring picture of a gifted and industrious woman of God.

While reading Proverbs, we should bear in mind that the sayings are not promises. Rather, they are principles for wise living. Although they provide the foundation for how God's people can flourish when they follow his wisdom, we live in a fallen world and therefore will experience exceptions to the rule. Other books in the biblical Wisdom genre—Job and Ecclesiastes—explore those exceptions as they grapple with the problem of evil and the mystery of suffering.

In this book, writers from *Our Daily Bread* guide us through each chapter of Proverbs with the Bible text included next to the day's devotional entry. Through the compelling stories, the Hebrew word studies and biblical insights, and of course the Scripture itself, you can unearth the riches of this ancient book and experience God's transforming wisdom. May your love for God deepen as you grow in your understanding of his wisdom for daily life.

—Amy Boucher Pye

Proverbs 1

¹ *The proverbs of Solomon son of David, king of Israel:*

² for gaining wisdom and instruction;
  for understanding words of insight;
³ for receiving instruction in prudent behavior,
  doing what is right and just and fair;
⁴ for giving prudence to those who are simple,
  knowledge and discretion to the young—
⁵ let the wise listen and add to their learning,
  and let the discerning get guidance—
⁶ for understanding proverbs and parables,
  the sayings and riddles of the wise.

⁷ The fear of the LORD is the beginning of knowledge,
  but fools despise wisdom and instruction.

⁸ Listen, my son, to your father's instruction
  and do not forsake your mother's teaching.
⁹ They are a garland to grace your head
  and a chain to adorn your neck.

¹⁰ My son, if sinful men entice you,
   do not give in to them.
¹¹ If they say, "Come along with us;
   let's lie in wait for innocent blood,
   let's ambush some harmless soul;
¹² let's swallow them alive, like the grave,
   and whole, like those who go down to the
      pit;
¹³ we will get all sorts of valuable things
   and fill our houses with plunder;
¹⁴ cast lots with us;
   we will all share the loot"—
¹⁵ my son, do not go along with them,
   do not set foot on their paths;
¹⁶ for their feet rush into evil,
   they are swift to shed blood.
¹⁷ How useless to spread a net
   where every bird can see it!
¹⁸ These men lie in wait for their own blood;
   they ambush only themselves!
¹⁹ Such are the paths of all who go after
      ill-gotten gain;
   it takes away the life of those who get it.

²⁰ Out in the open wisdom calls aloud,
   she raises her voice in the public square;
²¹ on top of the wall she cries out,
   at the city gate she makes her speech:

²² "How long will you who are simple love
      your simple ways?
   How long will mockers delight in mockery
   and fools hate knowledge?
²³ Repent at my rebuke!
   Then I will pour out my thoughts to you,
   I will make known to you my teachings.

²⁴ But since you refuse to listen when I call
   and no one pays attention when I stretch
      out my hand,
²⁵ since you disregard all my advice
   and do not accept my rebuke,
²⁶ I in turn will laugh when disaster strikes
      you;
   I will mock when calamity overtakes you—
²⁷ when calamity overtakes you like a storm,
   when disaster sweeps over you like a
      whirlwind,
   when distress and trouble overwhelm you.

²⁸ "Then they will call to me but I will not
      answer;
   they will look for me but will not find me,
²⁹ since they hated knowledge
   and did not choose to fear the LORD.
³⁰ Since they would not accept my advice
   and spurned my rebuke,
³¹ they will eat the fruit of their ways
   and be filled with the fruit of their
      schemes.
³² For the waywardness of the simple will kill
      them,
   and the complacency of fools will destroy
      them;
³³ but whoever listens to me will live in safety
   and be at ease, without fear of harm."

9

A Message Necklace

−ELISA MORGAN

Fear of the LORD is the foundation of true knowledge.

PROVERBS 1:7 NLT

Ellen opened her mailbox and discovered a bulky envelope with her dear friend's return address. Just a few days prior, she'd shared a relational struggle with that friend. Curious, she unwrapped the package and found a colorful beaded necklace on a simple jute string. Attached was a card with a company's slogan, "Say it in Morse Code," and words translating the necklace's hidden and wise message, "Seek God's ways." Ellen smiled as she fastened it about her neck.

The book of Proverbs is a compilation of wise sayings—many penned by Solomon, who was acclaimed as the wisest man of his era (1 Kings 10:23). Its thirty-one chapters call the reader to listen to wisdom and avoid folly, starting with the core message of 1:7, "The fear of the LORD is the beginning of knowledge." Wisdom—knowing what to do when—comes from honoring God by seeking his ways. In the introductory verses, we read, "Listen when your father corrects you. Don't neglect your mother's instruction. What you learn from them will crown you with grace and be a chain of honor around your neck" (Proverbs 1:8–9 NLT).

Ellen's friend had directed her to the Source of the wisdom she needed: Seek God's ways. Her gift focused Ellen's attention on where to discover the help she needed.

When we honor God and seek his ways, we'll receive the wisdom we need for all the matters we face in life. Each and every one. 🕊

What does wisdom mean to you?

Where do you go when you need guidance and wisdom?

INTRODUCING PROVERBS

The Proverbs are a collection of wise sayings to guide us through the choices and life decisions we face. The majority of these are attributed to Solomon, whose wisdom was greater than "all the people of the East" (see 1 Kings 4:29–33). Ultimately, however, the Source of all wisdom is our wise God. And the good news is that he makes that wisdom available to us—not only in Scripture texts like today's reading from Proverbs, but also in response to our prayers. James says, "If any of you lacks wisdom, you should ask God, who gives generously to all without finding fault, and it will be given to you" (James 1:5). Wisdom is available, if we will only ask!

BEFRIENDING WISDOM

Meet the charismatic, brilliant, and refreshingly honest Woman Wisdom. In chapters 1 through 9, wisdom is personified as a woman. Through the metaphor of Woman Wisdom, we see the vitality of God's wisdom.

In chapter 1, she opens wide an invitation to you (vv. 20–23). Woman Wisdom promises to be the straight-talking, intuitive voice as you discern your way—helping you press on amid hardship and joy, disappointment and triumph (3:13–18). She asks for only one thing in return: that you accept her as she is, in all her breathtaking glory (8:32–36). Will you choose Wisdom?

———— PRAY ————

Jesus, around me are so many things vying for my attention: responsibilities, cares, the crises in the world and in my everyday life, constant interruptions. And the noise buzzing within my own head is sometimes just as loud. I desperately need to listen to your voice to help me find my way.

Help me to stop and listen to you. Give me the ability to distinguish between your voice, distractions, my agenda (or the agenda of others), and the lies of the Enemy. Without you, I cannot navigate my path. But with you, I find strength and courage to press in, and the wisdom to discern my next steps.

In Jesus's name, Amen.

Proverbs 2

¹*My son, if you accept my words*
　　　and store up my commands within you,
²turning your ear to wisdom
　　　and applying your heart to understanding—
³indeed, if you call out for insight
　　　and cry aloud for understanding,
⁴and if you look for it as for silver
　　　and search for it as for hidden treasure,
⁵then you will understand the fear of the Lord
　　　and find the knowledge of God.
⁶For the Lord gives wisdom;
　　　from his mouth come knowledge and understanding.
⁷He holds success in store for the upright,
　　　he is a shield to those whose walk is blameless,
⁸for he guards the course of the just
　　　and protects the way of his faithful ones.

⁹ Then you will understand what is right and just
   and fair—every good path.
¹⁰ For wisdom will enter your heart,
   and knowledge will be pleasant to your soul.
¹¹ Discretion will protect you,
   and understanding will guard you.

¹² Wisdom will save you from the ways of wicked men,
   from men whose words are perverse,
¹³ who have left the straight paths
   to walk in dark ways,
¹⁴ who delight in doing wrong
   and rejoice in the perverseness of evil,
¹⁵ whose paths are crooked
   and who are devious in their ways.

¹⁶ Wisdom will save you also from the adulterous woman,
   from the wayward woman with her seductive words,
¹⁷ who has left the partner of her youth
   and ignored the covenant she made before God.
¹⁸ Surely her house leads down to death
   and her paths to the spirits of the dead.
¹⁹ None who go to her return
   or attain the paths of life.

²⁰ Thus you will walk in the ways of the good
   and keep to the paths of the righteous.
²¹ For the upright will live in the land,
   and the blameless will remain in it;
²² but the wicked will be cut off from the land,
   and the unfaithful will be torn from it. ❧

Missing: Wisdom

—ANNE CETAS

Understand the fear of the LORD
and find the knowledge of God.

PROVERBS 2:5

Two-year-old Kenneth went missing. Yet within three minutes of his mom's 9-1-1 call, an emergency worker found him just two blocks from home at the county fair. His mom had promised he could go later that day with his grandpa. But he'd driven his toy tractor there, and parked it at his favorite ride. When the boy was safely home, his dad wisely removed the toy's battery.

Kenneth was actually rather smart to get where he wanted to go, but two-year-olds are missing another key quality: wisdom. And as adults we sometimes lack it too. Solomon, who'd been appointed king by his father David (1 Kings 2), admitted he felt like a child. God appeared to him in a dream and said, "Ask for whatever you want me to give you" (3:5). He replied, "I am only a little child and do not know how to carry out my duties. . . . So give your servant a discerning heart to govern your people and to distinguish between right and wrong" (vv. 7, 9). God gave Solomon "a breadth of understanding as measureless as the sand on the seashore" (4:29).

Where can we get the wisdom we need? Solomon said the beginning of wisdom is a "fear" or awe of God (Proverbs 9:10). So we can start by asking him to teach us about himself and to give us wisdom beyond our own. 🌱

WISDOM

[chokmah] (v. 2)

In the Old Testament, *wisdom (chokmah* in Hebrew) can refer to vocational skills. For example, God called a master artisan, someone he specially filled with his Spirit and wisdom, to build the tabernacle (Exodus 31:6). Within the book of Proverbs, *chokmah* has a more expansive meaning, one we might define as the "skill of living."* To live with wisdom is to live in tune with God's Spirit in such a way that we make healthy, life-giving choices that, ultimately, bring glory to God. As God is the Source of all wisdom, Proverbs emphasizes that we can only uncover wisdom through seeking our Creator (9:10). When we humbly follow him, God gives us the grace, insight, and courage to face life's challenges and choices.

---

* Tremper Longman III, *How to Read Proverbs* (Downers Grover, IL: InterVarsity Press, 2002), chap. 1, Kindle

In what areas of your life do you need God's wisdom? Take time to express your needs to God— and listen for his response to you.

PROVERBS: AUTHORSHIP

In the first verse of Proverbs, the celebrated King Solomon is identified in an editorial role: "These are the proverbs of Solomon, David's son, king of Israel" (NLT). The sage famous for his incredible wisdom (1 Kings 4:31; 10:1–23) could have assembled the entire book; however, many scholars believe Solomon more likely edited some of it and wrote chapters 10–22:16 and 25–29:27—those showcasing the pithy proverbs for which the book is known. Why? Completed over hundreds of years, the book is speculated to have had a variety of compilers, including scribes from Hezekiah's court (see 25:1), and at least two other authors, Agur and King Lemuel (see chapters 30–31). Throughout this book, we refer to the author of Proverbs as Solomon for the sake of simplicity, with the understanding that others have been involved in the book's editing and writing.

Today's devotional says God wants to reveal himself to us personally. What would you like to know about him and his character? Take time to ask him now, and listen to his response to you.

15

Proverbs 3

¹ *My son, do not forget my teaching,*
> but keep my commands in your heart,
> ² for they will prolong your life many years
> and bring you peace and prosperity.

> ³ Let love and faithfulness never leave you;
> bind them around your neck,
> write them on the tablet of your heart.
> ⁴ Then you will win favor and a good name
> in the sight of God and man.

> ⁵ Trust in the LORD with all your heart
> and lean not on your own understanding;
> ⁶ in all your ways submit to him,
> and he will make your paths straight.

> ⁷ Do not be wise in your own eyes;
> fear the LORD and shun evil.
> ⁸ This will bring health to your body
> and nourishment to your bones.

⁹ Honor the LORD with your wealth,
    with the firstfruits of all your crops;
¹⁰ then your barns will be filled to overflowing,
    and your vats will brim over with new wine.
¹¹ My son, do not despise the LORD's discipline,
    and do not resent his rebuke,
¹² because the LORD disciplines those he loves,
    as a father the son he delights in.
¹³ Blessed are those who find wisdom,
    those who gain understanding,
¹⁴ for she is more profitable than silver
    and yields better returns than gold.
¹⁵ She is more precious than rubies;
    nothing you desire can compare with her.
¹⁶ Long life is in her right hand;
    in her left hand are riches and honor.
¹⁷ Her ways are pleasant ways,
    and all her paths are peace.
¹⁸ She is a tree of life to those who take hold
        of her;
    those who hold her fast will be blessed.
¹⁹ By wisdom the LORD laid the earth's
        foundations,
    by understanding he set the heavens in
        place;
²⁰ by his knowledge the watery depths were
        divided,
    and the clouds let drop the dew.
²¹ My son, do not let wisdom and
        understanding out of your sight,
    preserve sound judgment and discretion;
²² they will be life for you,
    an ornament to grace your neck.
²³ Then you will go on your way in safety,
    and your foot will not stumble.

²⁴ When you lie down, you will not be afraid;
    when you lie down, your sleep will be sweet.
²⁵ Have no fear of sudden disaster
    or of the ruin that overtakes the wicked,
²⁶ for the LORD will be at your side
    and will keep your foot from being snared.

²⁷ Do not withhold good from those to whom
        it is due,
    when it is in your power to act.
²⁸ Do not say to your neighbor,
    "Come back tomorrow and I'll give it to
        you"—
    when you already have it with you.
²⁹ Do not plot harm against your neighbor,
    who lives trustfully near you.
³⁰ Do not accuse anyone for no reason—
    when they have done you no harm.

³¹ Do not envy the violent
    or choose any of their ways.

³² For the LORD detests the perverse
    but takes the upright into his confidence.
³³ The LORD's curse is on the house of the
        wicked,
    but he blesses the home of the righteous.
³⁴ He mocks proud mockers
    but shows favor to the humble and
        oppressed.
³⁵ The wise inherit honor,
    but fools get only shame. ❧

Advice from My Father

—LINDA WASHINGTON

Trust in the LORD with all your heart
and lean not on your own understanding.

PROVERBS 3:5

After being laid off from an editorial job, I prayed, asking for God to help me find a new one. But when weeks went by and nothing came of my attempts at networking and filling out applications, I began to pout. "Don't you know how important it is that I have a job?" I asked God, my arms folded in protest at my seemingly unanswered prayer.

When I talked to my father, who had often reminded me about believing God's promises, about my job situation, he said, "I want you to get to the point where you trust what God says."

My father's advice reminds me of Proverbs 3, which includes wise advice from a parent to a beloved child. This familiar passage was especially applicable to my situation: "Trust in the LORD with all your heart and lean not on your own understanding; in all your ways submit to him, and he will make your paths straight" (vv. 5–6). To "make . . . paths straight" means God will guide us toward his goals for our growth. His ultimate goal is that I become more like him.

This does not mean that the paths he chooses will be easy. But I can choose to trust that his direction and timing are ultimately for my good.

Are you waiting on God for an answer? Choose to draw near to him and trust that he will guide you. 🐚

THE PATH IN PROVERBS

Today's reading says, "Trust in the Lord . . . and he will make your *paths* straight" (vv. 5–6, italics added). Throughout Proverbs, we're called to evaluate our life's *path*, that is, to wisely consider our choices. The repeated question in Proverbs is, Will you choose the path of wisdom leading to life, or the way of ignorance ending in death?

The motif of selecting a safe path would have been relevant in ancient Israel. To the Israelites who commuted by foot, navigation was a life-saving skill. They needed to identify and avoid hazardous roads—vulnerable to thieves, wild animals, or sudden drop-offs—to get home safely.

As you read, pay attention to the many references to *journeys* or *paths* in the first nine chapters of Proverbs.

TRUST [*batach*] (v. 5)
Through the invitation to *trust* in Proverbs 3:5, God promises us rest. The word *trust* (*batach* in Hebrew) is likely related to lying flat on your belly.* What a vulnerable position! For example, the psalmist in Psalm 22:9 compares *trust* to a newborn lying—fully loved, yet entirely helpless—at his mother's chest. *Trust* in Proverbs 3:5 seems to point to this same picture of vulnerably resting on something or someone else—an invitation, then, to lean like a child on our strong Father, releasing our future into his capable hands.†

Name and identify an area in which you struggle to trust God. Share that with him in prayer.

Where do you need God to move on your behalf? Talk with him about it.

How has he shown up for you in the past? Take time to praise him for his faithfulness to you.

---

* "Difficult Words in the Hebrew Prophets," *Studies in Old Testament Prophecy*, ed. H. H. Rowley (Edinburgh: T. & T. Clark, 1950), 59, cited in Derek Kidner, *Proverbs: An Introduction and Commentary* (Downers Grove, IL: InterVarsity, 2008), 61.

† Derek Kidner, *Proverbs: An Introduction and Commentary* (Downers Grove, IL: InterVarsity, 2008), 61.

PROVERBS: AUDIENCE

Originally, Proverbs was guidance for a teenage boy. In chapters 1 through 9, pay attention to how Solomon addresses it to his "son" (or, on occasion, "sons"). In ancient court traditions, kings like Solomon would write texts on wise living for their royal sons or students whom they called sons. In either case, they wanted to raise up discerning young men for leadership. (Excluded from this leadership track were women, who did not go to school.) Throughout the first nine chapters, the father figure Solomon tells his teenage son or pupil, if he learns nothing else, he should remember this: wisdom begins in worship (9:10).

Proverbs 4

¹ *Listen, my sons, to a father's instruction;*
> pay attention and gain understanding.
² I give you sound learning,
> so do not forsake my teaching.
³ For I too was a son to my father,
> still tender, and cherished by my mother.
⁴ Then he taught me, and he said to me,
> "Take hold of my words with all your heart;
> keep my commands, and you will live.
⁵ Get wisdom, get understanding;
> do not forget my words or turn away from them.
⁶ Do not forsake wisdom, and she will protect you;
> love her, and she will watch over you.
⁷ The beginning of wisdom is this: Get wisdom.
> Though it cost all you have, get understanding.
⁸ Cherish her, and she will exalt you;
> embrace her, and she will honor you.
⁹ She will give you a garland to grace your head
> and present you with a glorious crown."

¹⁰ Listen, my son, accept what I say,
   and the years of your life will be many.
¹¹ I instruct you in the way of wisdom
   and lead you along straight paths.
¹² When you walk, your steps will not be hampered;
   when you run, you will not stumble.
¹³ Hold on to instruction, do not let it go;
   guard it well, for it is your life.
¹⁴ Do not set foot on the path of the wicked
   or walk in the way of evildoers.
¹⁵ Avoid it, do not travel on it;
   turn from it and go on your way.
¹⁶ For they cannot rest until they do evil;
   they are robbed of sleep till they make someone stumble.
¹⁷ They eat the bread of wickedness
   and drink the wine of violence.

¹⁸ The path of the righteous is like the morning sun,
   shining ever brighter till the full light of day.
¹⁹ But the way of the wicked is like deep darkness;
   they do not know what makes them stumble.
²⁰ My son, pay attention to what I say;
   turn your ear to my words.
²¹ Do not let them out of your sight,
   keep them within your heart;
²² for they are life to those who find them
   and health to one's whole body.
²³ Above all else, guard your heart,
   for everything you do flows from it.
²⁴ Keep your mouth free of perversity;
   keep corrupt talk far from your lips.
²⁵ Let your eyes look straight ahead;
   fix your gaze directly before you.
²⁶ Give careful thought to the paths for your feet
   and be steadfast in all your ways.
²⁷ Do not turn to the right or the left;
   keep your foot from evil.

Heart Matters

–POH FANG CHIA

Above all else, guard your heart,
for everything you do flows from it.

PROVERBS 4:23

In the devotional, the author observes that "life will always make demands upon our time and energy that cry out for immediate attention." What demands in your own life are "crying out for your attention"? Are these demands helping you focus on what matters most to you? Why or why not?

Our hearts pump at a rate of 70 to 75 beats per minute. Though weighing only 11 ounces on average, a healthy heart pumps 2,000 gallons of blood through 60,000 miles of blood vessels each day. Every day, the heart creates enough energy to drive a truck 20 miles. In a lifetime, that is equivalent to driving to the moon and back. A healthy heart can do amazing things. Conversely, if our heart malfunctions, our whole body shuts down.

The same could be said of our spiritual heart. In Scripture, the word *heart* represents the center of our emotions, thinking, and reasoning. It is the command center of our life.

Have you ever had a "spiritual heart attack"? What led to it?

So when we read, "Keep your heart with all diligence" (Proverbs 4:23 NKJV), it makes a lot of sense. But it's difficult advice to keep. Life will always make demands upon our time and energy that cry out for immediate attention. By comparison, taking time to hear God's Word and to do what it says may not shout quite so loudly. We may not notice the consequences of neglect right away, but over time it may give way to a spiritual heart attack.

I'm thankful God has given us his Word. We need his help not to neglect it, but to use it to align our hearts with his every day. 🝔

What does it look like for you to "keep your heart with all diligence" (v. 23)?

HEART

[leb, lebab] (v. 23) Has someone *broken your heart*? Or maybe you were the one to *steal someone's heart*? Now, our hearts aren't really being fractured, and we're not in the business of hijacking hearts. So, what do we really mean? In our culture, the physical heart is a metaphor for the place we experience our emotions. The ancient Israelites also saw the physical heart as the center of emotion. To them, though, the heart was also like our idea of the brain—the center of thought. From the secret places of the heart, we cooked up schemes (both good and evil!), dreamed up ideas, and conceived our deepest desires (6:18; 16:9; 4:23). Ultimately, it was the place we made our choices. That's why the writers of Proverbs call us to safeguard the heart—for "everything [we] do flows from it" (4:23).

PROVERBS: STRUCTURE

The book of Proverbs comprises three parts. In chapters 1 through 9, King Solomon shares his heart with his son or disciple, encouraging him to walk wisely by pursuing a relationship with his Creator (9:10). Following this series of encouragements, the second part of the book, chapters 10 through 29, contains the proverbs that make it famous. The last two chapters form the conclusion—culminating in a celebration of a woman of strength in Proverbs 31.

Proverbs 5

¹*My son, pay attention to my wisdom,*

turn your ear to my words of insight,
²that you may maintain discretion
and your lips may preserve knowledge.
³For the lips of the adulterous woman drip honey,
and her speech is smoother than oil;
⁴but in the end she is bitter as gall,
sharp as a double-edged sword.
⁵Her feet go down to death;
her steps lead straight to the grave.
⁶She gives no thought to the way of life;
her paths wander aimlessly, but she does not know it.

⁷ Now then, my sons, listen to me;
  do not turn aside from what I say.
⁸ Keep to a path far from her,
  do not go near the door of her house,
⁹ lest you lose your honor to others
  and your dignity to one who is cruel,
¹⁰ lest strangers feast on your wealth
  and your toil enrich the house of another.
¹¹ At the end of your life you will groan,
  when your flesh and body are spent.
¹² You will say, "How I hated discipline!
  How my heart spurned correction!
¹³ I would not obey my teachers
  or turn my ear to my instructors.
¹⁴ And I was soon in serious trouble
  in the assembly of God's people."

¹⁵ Drink water from your own cistern,
  running water from your own well.
¹⁶ Should your springs overflow in the streets,
  your streams of water in the public squares?
¹⁷ Let them be yours alone,
  never to be shared with strangers.
¹⁸ May your fountain be blessed,
  and may you rejoice in the wife of your youth.
¹⁹ A loving doe, a graceful deer—
  may her breasts satisfy you always,
  may you ever be intoxicated with her love.
²⁰ Why, my son, be intoxicated with another man's wife?
  Why embrace the bosom of a wayward woman?

²¹ For your ways are in full view of the LORD,
  and he examines all your paths.
²² The evil deeds of the wicked ensnare them;
  the cords of their sins hold them fast.
²³ For lack of discipline they will die,
  led astray by their own great folly. ❧

The Beauty of Love

—KEILA OCHOA

May your fountain be blessed.

PROVERBS 5:18

The "Jarabe Tapatío," also known as the Mexican hat dance, celebrates romance. During this upbeat dance, the man places his sombrero on the ground. At the very end, the woman grabs the hat and both hide behind it to seal their romance with a kiss.

This dance reminds me of the importance of faithfulness. In Proverbs 5, after talking about the high cost of immorality, we find imagery vividly depicting the exclusivity of marriage: "Drink water from your own cistern, running water from your own well" (v. 15). Even with ten couples dancing the Jarabe on stage, each person focuses on his or her partner. We can rejoice in deep and undivided commitment between spouses (v. 18).

The romance is also being observed. The dancers, while they are enjoying their partner, know there is an audience. In the same way, we read, "For your ways are in full view of the LORD, and he examines all your paths" (v. 21). God wants to protect our relationships, and he's constantly watching us. May we please him through the loyalty we show to each other.

Just like in the Jarabe, there is a rhythm to follow in life. When we keep the beat of our Creator by being faithful to him—whether we are married or unmarried—we find blessings and joy. 🌿

In what ways are you cultivating healthy relationships?

What boundaries have you set to protect the relationships that matter most to you?

What truths from today's Bible reading or devotional resonate with you?

ON SEX AND MARRIAGE

In today's Bible passage, we reflect on the gifts of marriage—and the dangers of seeking its pleasures elsewhere. While marriage serves many practical purposes, it was also created for pleasure—*God delights in the beauty of sex and intimacy* (vv. 15–20)! Here, the author, who is instructing his son or disciple, encourages him to celebrate marriage and embrace the joys of sex (vv. 18–19). Embedded within this passage, though, is a warning: *beware of the dangers of sexual love outside of marriage* (vv. 4–6). The father admits that forbidden romance can be alluring, at least initially. Once the thrills have waned, however, there remain devastating, far-reaching consequences (vv. 22–23).

WARNING TO A YOUNG PERSON

If you were writing a letter to someone of the next generation, what pitfalls would you caution him or her against? In Proverbs, Solomon repeatedly warns his teenage son or student of the temptation of an illicit relationship. That's why here and elsewhere we encounter the "adulterous woman" (2:16–22; 6:20–35, most of chapters 5 and 7). The word translated "adulterous" means *foreign* in Hebrew. She is *foreign* because her behavior to engage in extramarital sex was foreign or alien—that is, deviant. In the descriptions, her words "drip honey"; her pledge of pleasure is seductive (5:3). But the lesson Solomon wants to get across to this teenager? An affair promises tantalizing satisfaction but will wreck a young adult's life before it has barely begun.

The recurring figure of this adulterous woman also points to a larger motif in the book, that of the choice to be made between the paths of Wisdom and Folly. In this context, the adulterous woman can be seen as a contrast to Woman Wisdom, and falling for her seduction is a metaphor for abandoning Woman Wisdom for the path of folly.

—PRAY—

Jesus, thank you for caring for my loved ones. Give them a spirit attuned to you, a discerning mind to discriminate between truth and lies, and a humble, teachable heart. Most of all, help them experience your extravagant, tender love for them.

Thank you for your nearness, the way you support me in my relationships (Matthew 18:20). Where you are, there is power. I desperately need you to love well. Help me have unity of purpose and vision with those I love, especially when we are exhausted, busy, and disconnected from each other. Heal the broken places within our relationship, where resentment, ungratefulness, and frustration take root. Equip us to build the foundation of our relationship on your ways and the values of your kingdom (Matthew 6:33).

Protect us from the Enemy, who likes to sow discord, chaos, and division—within me, within my family, and among my friends. Give us the awareness of—and the ability to put on—your armor, which you've given us for defense and offense against the Enemy (Ephesians 6:10–18). I thank you that you arm us for battle and go before us, behind us, that in you we find sanctuary, peace, and victory.

In Jesus's name, Amen.

Proverbs 6

¹ *My son, if you have put up security for your neighbor,*
   if you have shaken hands in pledge for a stranger,
² you have been trapped by what you said,
   ensnared by the words of your mouth.
³ So do this, my son, to free yourself,
   since you have fallen into your neighbor's hands:
Go—to the point of exhaustion—
   and give your neighbor no rest!
⁴ Allow no sleep to your eyes,
   no slumber to your eyelids.
⁵ Free yourself, like a gazelle from the hand of the hunter,
   like a bird from the snare of the fowler.

⁶ Go to the ant, you sluggard;
   consider its ways and be wise!
⁷ It has no commander,
   no overseer or ruler,
⁸ yet it stores its provisions in summer
   and gathers its food at harvest.

⁹ How long will you lie there, you sluggard?
   When will you get up from your sleep?
¹⁰ A little sleep, a little slumber,
   a little folding of the hands to rest—
¹¹ and poverty will come on you like a thief
   and scarcity like an armed man.

¹² A troublemaker and a villain,
   who goes about with a corrupt mouth,
   ¹³ who winks maliciously with his eye,
   signals with his feet
   and motions with his fingers,
   ¹⁴ who plots evil with deceit in his heart—
   he always stirs up conflict.
¹⁵ Therefore disaster will overtake him in an instant;
   he will suddenly be destroyed—without remedy.

¹⁶ There are six things the LORD hates,
   seven that are detestable to him:
      ¹⁷ haughty eyes,
      a lying tongue,
      hands that shed innocent blood,
      ¹⁸ a heart that devises wicked schemes,
      feet that are quick to rush into evil,
      ¹⁹ a false witness who pours out lies
      and a person who stirs up conflict in the community.

²⁰ My son, keep your father's command
   and do not forsake your mother's teaching.
²¹ Bind them always on your heart;
   fasten them around your neck.
²² When you walk, they will guide you;
   when you sleep, they will watch over you;
   when you awake, they will speak to you.
²³ For this command is a lamp,
   this teaching is a light,
and correction and instruction
   are the way to life,
²⁴ keeping you from your neighbor's wife,
   from the smooth talk of a wayward woman.

²⁵ Do not lust in your heart after her beauty
   or let her captivate you with her eyes.

²⁶ For a prostitute can be had for a loaf of bread,
   but another man's wife preys on your very life.
²⁷ Can a man scoop fire into his lap
   without his clothes being burned?
²⁸ Can a man walk on hot coals
   without his feet being scorched?
²⁹ So is he who sleeps with another man's wife;
   no one who touches her will go unpunished.

³⁰ People do not despise a thief if he steals
   to satisfy his hunger when he is starving.
³¹ Yet if he is caught, he must pay sevenfold,
   though it costs him all the wealth of his house.
³² But a man who commits adultery has no sense;
   whoever does so destroys himself.
³³ Blows and disgrace are his lot,
   and his shame will never be wiped away.

³⁴ For jealousy arouses a husband's fury,
   and he will show no mercy when he takes revenge.
³⁵ He will not accept any compensation;
   he will refuse a bribe, however great it is. ❧

The Wise Ant

—JENNIFER BENSON SCHULDT

The ant . . . stores its provisions in summer
and gathers its food at harvest.

PROVERBS 6:6–8

Every year I do something special to celebrate the arrival of spring—I buy ant traps. Those little invaders continually march into our kitchen in search of any crumb left on the floor. They aren't picky; a shard of potato chip, a grain of rice, or even a speck of cheese will do.

Although ants may be a nuisance, Solomon praised them for their steadfast work ethic (Proverbs 6:6–11). He pointed out that ants are self-directed. They have no captain, commander, or ruler (v. 7), yet they are very productive. The ants also keep busy even when it's not immediately necessary, providing supplies in the summer and gathering food in the harvest (v. 8). By the time winter arrives, they're not worried about what they will eat. Little by little, these hard workers have saved up enough to sustain themselves.

We can learn from the ant. When God gives us times of plenty, we can prepare for times when resources may be low. God is the provider of all that we have, including our ability to work. We are to work diligently, be wise stewards of what he has provided, and then rest in the promise of his care (Matthew 6:25–34).

Let's remember Solomon's advice: "Go to the ant . . . ; consider its ways and be wise" (Proverbs 6:6).

PROVERBS: SCOPE

The book of Proverbs helps us theologically, practically, and ethically. It helps us theologically by describing the nature of wisdom as centered in God, practically by guiding us toward skillful living, and ethically by showing us how to live both individually and in community.

Some of the many practical topics that guide us toward wise living include family relationships (6:20), sexual ethics (6:23–29), taking care of the poor (14:21; 19:17; 28:27), listening to advice (9:7–9), work ethics (10:4–5), business ethics (11:1, 26), life planning (16:1–3, 9, 33), dealing with authority (23:1–3), relationships with friends and neighbors (24:28–29; 27:14), avoiding conflict (26:17, 20–21), the pitfalls of anger (29:22), and the danger of pride (29:23).*

* Adapted from Tremper Longman III, Understanding the Bible: The Wisdom Books (Discovery Series, Our Daily Bread Ministries), https://discoveryseries.org/courses/understanding-the-bible-the-wisdom-books/lessons/introduction-42/.

Are you a natural planner? Or do you prefer improvising and living more spontaneously?

How is God asking you to diligently steward a task or responsibility right now?

In what ways are you being called to plan and prepare for the future?

AUTHOR BIOGRAPHY: KING SOLOMON

Wisdom was King Solomon's life quest. When the son of David became king, he humbly asked God for a "discerning heart" to lead the people of Israel, and God made him "wiser than anyone else" (1 Kings 3:9; 4:31). Famous for his understanding, Solomon attracted the attention of world leaders—like the queen of Sheba—who traveled to his court to learn from him (1 Kings 10:1–23).

While an extraordinary leader, Solomon has a complicated legacy. Along his life's path, he abandoned the core message he preaches throughout Proverbs—that true wisdom begins in pursuing God wholeheartedly (Proverbs 9:10). As an eminent king, he had many foreign wives from different religious backgrounds who "turned his heart after other gods" (1 Kings 11:4). It is through this brilliant yet deeply flawed leader, however, that we receive an exquisite inheritance: In books like Proverbs, Song of Songs, and Ecclesiastes, he has liberally offered his genius to us—gifts of wisdom, matchless insight into human nature, and admiration for and celebrations of beauty, unparalleled in all of Scripture. We are indebted to this exceptional, complex king of Israel.

Proverbs 7

¹*My son, keep my words*
  and store up my commands within you.
²Keep my commands and you will live;
  guard my teachings as the apple of your eye.
³Bind them on your fingers;
  write them on the tablet of your heart.
⁴Say to wisdom, "You are my sister,"
  and to insight, "You are my relative."
⁵They will keep you from the adulterous woman,
  from the wayward woman with her seductive words.

⁶At the window of my house
  I looked down through the lattice.
⁷I saw among the simple,
  I noticed among the young men,
  a youth who had no sense.
⁸He was going down the street near her corner,
  walking along in the direction of her house
⁹at twilight, as the day was fading,
  as the dark of night set in.

¹⁰ Then out came a woman to meet him,
dressed like a prostitute and with crafty
intent.
¹¹ (She is unruly and defiant,
her feet never stay at home;
¹² now in the street, now in the squares,
at every corner she lurks.)
¹³ She took hold of him and kissed him
and with a brazen face she said:

¹⁴ "Today I fulfilled my vows,
and I have food from my fellowship
offering at home.
¹⁵ So I came out to meet you;
I looked for you and have found you!
¹⁶ I have covered my bed
with colored linens from Egypt.
¹⁷ I have perfumed my bed
with myrrh, aloes and cinnamon.
¹⁸ Come, let's drink deeply of love till morning;
let's enjoy ourselves with love!
¹⁹ My husband is not at home;
he has gone on a long journey.

²⁰ He took his purse filled with money
and will not be home till full moon."

²¹ With persuasive words she led him astray;
she seduced him with her smooth talk.
²² All at once he followed her
like an ox going to the slaughter,
like a deer stepping into a noose
²³ till an arrow pierces his liver,
like a bird darting into a snare,
little knowing it will cost him his life.

²⁴ Now then, my sons, listen to me;
pay attention to what I say.
²⁵ Do not let your heart turn to her ways
or stray into her paths.
²⁶ Many are the victims she has brought down;
her slain are a mighty throng.
²⁷ Her house is a highway to the grave,
leading down to the chambers of death.

Printed on Our Hearts

—KIRSTEN HOLMBERG

Bind them on your fingers;
write them on the tablet of your heart.

PROVERBS 7:3

When Johannes Gutenberg combined the printing press with moveable type in 1450, he ushered in the era of mass communications in the West, spreading learning into new social realms. Literacy increased across the globe and new ideas produced rapid transformations in social and religious contexts. Gutenberg produced the first-ever printed version of the Bible. Prior to this, Bibles were painstakingly hand-copied, taking scribes up to a year to produce.

For centuries since, the printing press has provided people like you and me the privilege of direct access to Scripture. While we also have electronic versions available to us, many of us often hold a physical Bible in our hands because of his invention. What was once inaccessible given the sheer cost and time to have a Bible copied is readily at our fingertips today.

Having access to God's truth is an amazing privilege. The writer of Proverbs indicates we should treat his instructions to us in the Scriptures as something to be cherished, as "the apple of [our] eye" (Proverbs 7:2) and to write his words of wisdom on "the tablet of [our] heart" (v. 3). As we seek to understand the Bible and live according to its wisdom, we, like scribes, are drawing God's truth from our "fingers" down into our hearts, to be taken with us wherever we go. 🕊

How has having Scripture stored in your heart benefited you?

How can you begin to internalize more of God's wisdom?

BIND [qashar] (v. 3)

When we're instructed to "bind" (*qashar*) the teacher's words on our fingers and "on the tablet of [our] heart" (Proverbs 7:3), the image is that of an inseparable bond. In Genesis 43:30, for example, this same word is used by Judah to explain to Joseph why he cannot leave Benjamin; his father Jacob's life was so "bound up with the boy's life" that separation would cause him to die of grief.

In the Jewish faith, the idea of binding wisdom into one's heart was sometimes captured by literally binding tefillin or phylacteries—small leather boxes containing parchment with verses from the Torah—to one's arms or forehead. To live in God's world with wisdom requires us to so internalize divine truth that it becomes inseparable from our own hearts.

MEET "THE SIMPLE" (v. 7)

Throughout Proverbs, we bump into "the simple" character or group (first in 1:22). So, who are "the simple" in Proverbs? First, the word for *simple* (*pthiy* in Hebrew) means someone naïve, inexperienced. Imagine an idealistic teenager whose tremendous energy can be channeled for great purpose or destruction, and you have a pretty good grasp of this gullible, usually lovable, and sometimes-blundering person or group in Proverbs. Unlike the foolish character we encounter in the book, the simple can learn. If they don't, however, they will by default walk the way of the fool—to their detriment (case in point: the man "among the simple" in today's Bible reading).

The simple desperately need a mentor (and maybe a healthy peer group too). The author of Proverbs says that the book is to serve as one such mentor (1:4).

Proverbs 8

¹ *Does not wisdom call out?*
　　Does not understanding raise her voice?
² At the highest point along the way,
　　where the paths meet, she takes her stand;
³ beside the gate leading into the city,
　　at the entrance, she cries aloud:
⁴ "To you, O people, I call out;
　　I raise my voice to all mankind.
⁵ You who are simple, gain prudence;
　　you who are foolish, set your hearts on it.
⁶ Listen, for I have trustworthy things to say;
　　I open my lips to speak what is right.
⁷ My mouth speaks what is true,
　　for my lips detest wickedness.
⁸ All the words of my mouth are just;
　　none of them is crooked or perverse.
⁹ To the discerning all of them are right;
　　they are upright to those who have found knowledge.

¹⁰ Choose my instruction instead of silver,
  knowledge rather than choice gold,
¹¹ for wisdom is more precious than rubies,
  and nothing you desire can compare with her.

¹² "I, wisdom, dwell together with prudence;
  I possess knowledge and discretion.
¹³ To fear the LORD is to hate evil;
  I hate pride and arrogance,
  evil behavior and perverse speech.
¹⁴ Counsel and sound judgment are mine;
  I have insight, I have power.
¹⁵ By me kings reign
  and rulers issue decrees that are just;
¹⁶ by me princes govern,
  and nobles—all who rule on earth.
¹⁷ I love those who love me,
  and those who seek me find me.
¹⁸ With me are riches and honor,
  enduring wealth and prosperity.
¹⁹ My fruit is better than fine gold;
  what I yield surpasses choice silver.
²⁰ I walk in the way of righteousness,
  along the paths of justice,
²¹ bestowing a rich inheritance on those who love me
  and making their treasuries full.

²² "The LORD brought me forth as the first of his works,
   before his deeds of old;
²³ I was formed long ages ago,
   at the very beginning, when the world came to be.
²⁴ When there were no watery depths, I was given birth,
   when there were no springs overflowing with water;
²⁵ before the mountains were settled in place,
   before the hills, I was given birth,
²⁶ before he made the world or its fields
   or any of the dust of the earth.
²⁷ I was there when he set the heavens in place,
   when he marked out the horizon on the face of the deep,
²⁸ when he established the clouds above
   and fixed securely the fountains of the deep,
²⁹ when he gave the sea its boundary
   so the waters would not overstep his command,
and when he marked out the foundations of the earth.
   ³⁰ Then I was constantly at his side.
I was filled with delight day after day,
   rejoicing always in his presence,
³¹ rejoicing in his whole world
   and delighting in mankind.

³² "Now then, my children, listen to me;
   blessed are those who keep my ways.
³³ Listen to my instruction and be wise;
   do not disregard it.
³⁴ Blessed are those who listen to me,
   watching daily at my doors,
   waiting at my doorway.
³⁵ For those who find me find life
   and receive favor from the LORD.
³⁶ But those who fail to find me harm themselves;
   all who hate me love death." ❧

Wisdom's Call

—DAVID C. MCCASLAND

Wisdom is more precious than rubies,
and nothing you desire can compare with her.

PROVERBS 8:11

Malcolm Muggeridge, the noted British journalist and social critic, came to faith in Christ at the age of sixty. On his seventy-fifth birthday he offered twenty-five insightful observations about life. One said, "I never met a rich man who was happy, but I have only very occasionally met a poor man who did not want to become a rich man."

Most of us would agree that money can't make us happy, but we might like to have more so we can be sure.

God offers the true riches of wisdom to all who seek and follow him.

King Solomon's net worth has been estimated at more than two trillion US dollars. Although he was very wealthy, he knew that money had great limitations. Proverbs 8 is based on his experience and offers "Wisdom's Call" to all people. "I raise my voice to all mankind. . . . My mouth speaks what is true. . . .Choose my instruction instead of silver, knowledge rather than choice gold, for wisdom is more precious than rubies, and nothing you desire can compare with her" (vv. 4, 7, 10–11).

Wisdom says, "My fruit is better than fine gold; what I yield surpasses choice silver. I walk in the way of righteousness, along the paths of justice, bestowing a rich inheritance on those who love me and making their treasuries full" (vv. 19–21).

These are true riches indeed! ❧

WISDOM'S ROLE IN CREATION

In chapter 8, we meet Woman Wisdom again. In her longest monologue, she shares about her participation in the creation of the world (vv. 22–31). Wisdom was with God at the beginning, God's joyful accomplice in bringing about beauty, order, and creativity into all the earth. Through her speech, we discover that God's wisdom is woven into the fabric of the universe—and when we reject wisdom, we are at odds with the design God has purposed throughout time!

BROUGHT...FORTH

[qanah] (v. 22)

In the Old Testament, the word translated "brought . . . forth" in Proverbs 8 (qanah) often connects to pregnancy and childbirth. Consider the words of the mother of humanity, Eve. After contending with childbirth to deliver her firstborn, she cried out: "With the help of the LORD I have brought forth [qanah] a man" (Genesis 4:1). The word can also be rendered "acquired, created." In Proverbs 8, wisdom is said to have been conceived, formed (v. 22), and birthed (v. 24–25) at the world's beginnings. While the narrative is poetic—not to be taken literally—it's a beautiful celebration of wisdom's ancient origins.

In chapter 8, Woman Wisdom reveals many of the attributes of wisdom. What characteristics of wisdom surprise or are compelling to you? Why?

What are the true riches of wisdom?

—PRAY—

Jesus, I praise you for being the Master Artisan, threading wisdom into the very fabric of your created world (Proverbs 8:22–31).

When I stop to revel in the glory of the world around me, I glimpse your vast wisdom and power, leaving me in awe of you (Colossians 2:3).

How amazing that I serve a God who so meticulously layered beauty, harmony, and order into the foundation of the earth and beyond!

And you created me in your image—endowing me with the extraordinary power to create like you. I ask for boldness and wisdom to use my creativity— whether that is casting a vision for something entirely new; improving systems or structures in my job, at home, or in my community; or efficiently solving the myriad problems I face each day. Keep my mind sharp so that I am awake to what you want to do in and through me today.

In Jesus's name, Amen.

Proverbs 9

¹ *Wisdom has built her house;*

she has set up its seven pillars.
² She has prepared her meat and mixed her wine;
she has also set her table.
³ She has sent out her servants, and she calls
from the highest point of the city,
⁴ "Let all who are simple come to my house!"
To those who have no sense she says,
⁵ "Come, eat my food
and drink the wine I have mixed.
⁶ Leave your simple ways and you will live;
walk in the way of insight."

⁷ Whoever corrects a mocker invites insults;
whoever rebukes the wicked incurs abuse.
⁸ Do not rebuke mockers or they will hate you;
rebuke the wise and they will love you.
⁹ Instruct the wise and they will be wiser still;
teach the righteous and they will add to their learning.

[10] The fear of the Lord is the beginning of wisdom,
and knowledge of the Holy One is understanding.
[11] For through wisdom your days will be many,
and years will be added to your life.
[12] If you are wise, your wisdom will reward you;
if you are a mocker, you alone will suffer.

[13] Folly is an unruly woman;
she is simple and knows nothing.
[14] She sits at the door of her house,
on a seat at the highest point of the city,
[15] calling out to those who pass by,
who go straight on their way,
[16] "Let all who are simple come to my house!"
To those who have no sense she says,
[17] "Stolen water is sweet;
food eaten in secret is delicious!"
[18] But little do they know that the dead are there,
that her guests are deep in the realm of the dead.

True Fear

—AMY BOUCHER PYE

The fear of the LORD is the beginning of wisdom.

PROVERBS 9:10

Jeremy wrote, "I know quite a bit about the fear of dying. Seven years ago . . . I felt intense, sickening, dizzying, overwhelming fear when I was told I had incurable cancer." But he learned to manage his fear by leaning on the presence of God and moving from his fear of death to embracing "the fear of the LORD." To Jeremy, this meant being in awe of the Maker of the universe who will "swallow up death" (Isaiah 25:8) while also understanding deep within that God knows and loves him.

The fear of the Lord—a deep respect and awe for our holy God—is a theme that runs throughout Scripture. King Solomon admonished his son to fear the Lord in his series of wise sayings, the Proverbs. He said that if his son would turn his "ear to wisdom" and "search for it as for hidden treasure," then he'd "understand the fear of the LORD and find the knowledge of God" (Proverbs 2:2, 4, 5). Along with wisdom and knowledge, he'd find discretion and understanding (vv. 2:10–11; 9:10).

When we face challenges of many kinds and experience a sense of dread and fear, we're reminded of our limitations. But as we turn to God, asking him to help us humble ourselves before him and worship him in reverence, we'll find he helps us to move from being fearful to embracing a healthy fear of him. 🌿

FEAR

[*yirah*, from *yare*] (v. 10)
According to Proverbs, *the fear of the Lord* leads to discovering wisdom (1:7; 2:5; 9:10). In fact, the big idea of Proverbs could be summed up in that one simple phrase. In the Old Testament, *fear—awe—of God* will show itself in wholehearted worship of our Creator: giving ourselves to God in our decisions, actions, and attitudes (Deuteronomy 5:29; 8:6; 13:4). *Fear of God* is inseparable from the *knowledge of God—* namely, knowing him intimately (see Proverbs 2:5 and 9:10). Thus, it is only in a personal relationship with our Creator can we uncover true wisdom!

When you think of the word fear, *what comes to mind? Does it have a positive or negative connotation for you?*

insight

LIFE OR DEATH DECISION

Will we befriend Wisdom or Folly? In chapter 9, Woman Wisdom entreats us one final time—*Choose me, she says, and walk in the way of insight* (vv. 3–6). She makes every effort to impress, preparing a feast and inviting us to dinner (vv. 1–6). However, Wisdom has a beguiling rival—Folly, the personification of ignorance, who extends a dinner invitation of her own (vv. 13–18). While both have attractive offers, we'll make it out of only one of their homes alive (vv. 6, 18). The conclusion of the first section of Proverbs captures the book's motif: we can choose the way of Wisdom leading to life and favor (8:35), or the way of Folly causing devastation and death (v. 18). So, whose dinner invitation will you accept?

How important is the fear of God to you? How could you humble yourself before him today?

Proverbs 10

¹ *The proverbs of Solomon:*

A wise son brings joy to his father,
  but a foolish son brings grief to his mother.

² Ill-gotten treasures have no lasting value,
  but righteousness delivers from death.

³ The Lord does not let the righteous go hungry,
  but he thwarts the craving of the wicked.

⁴ Lazy hands make for poverty,
  but diligent hands bring wealth.

⁵ He who gathers crops in summer is a prudent son,
  but he who sleeps during harvest is a disgraceful son.

⁶ Blessings crown the head of the righteous,
  but violence overwhelms the mouth of the wicked.

⁷ The name of the righteous is used in blessings,
    but the name of the wicked will rot.

⁸ The wise in heart accept commands,
    but a chattering fool comes to ruin.

⁹ Whoever walks in integrity walks securely,
    but whoever takes crooked paths will be found out.

¹⁰ Whoever winks maliciously causes grief,
    and a chattering fool comes to ruin.

¹¹ The mouth of the righteous is a fountain of life,
    but the mouth of the wicked conceals violence.

¹² Hatred stirs up conflict,
    but love covers over all wrongs.

¹³ Wisdom is found on the lips of the discerning,
    but a rod is for the back of one who has no sense.

¹⁴ The wise store up knowledge,
    but the mouth of a fool invites ruin.

¹⁵ The wealth of the rich is their fortified city,
    but poverty is the ruin of the poor.

¹⁶ The wages of the righteous is life,
    but the earnings of the wicked are sin and death.

¹⁷ Whoever heeds discipline shows the way to life,
    but whoever ignores correction leads others astray.

¹⁸ Whoever conceals hatred with lying lips
    and spreads slander is a fool.

¹⁹ Sin is not ended by multiplying words,
    but the prudent hold their tongues.

²⁰ The tongue of the righteous is choice silver,
    but the heart of the wicked is of little value.

²¹ The lips of the righteous nourish many,
    but fools die for lack of sense.

²² The blessing of the LORD brings wealth,
    without painful toil for it.

²³ A fool finds pleasure in wicked schemes,
    but a person of understanding delights in wisdom.

²⁴ What the wicked dread will overtake them;
    what the righteous desire will be granted.

²⁵ When the storm has swept by, the wicked are gone,
  but the righteous stand firm forever.

²⁶ As vinegar to the teeth and smoke to the eyes,
  so are sluggards to those who send them.

²⁷ The fear of the LORD adds length to life,
  but the years of the wicked are cut short.

²⁸ The prospect of the righteous is joy,
  but the hopes of the wicked come to nothing.

²⁹ The way of the LORD is a refuge for the blameless,
  but it is the ruin of those who do evil.

³⁰ The righteous will never be uprooted,
  but the wicked will not remain in the land.

³¹ From the mouth of the righteous comes the fruit of wisdom,
  but a perverse tongue will be silenced.

³² The lips of the righteous know what finds favor,
  but the mouth of the wicked only what is perverse. ❧

Whispering Gallery

−BILL CROWDER

In the multitude of words sin is not lacking, but he who restrains his lips is wise.

PROVERBS 10:19 (NKJV)

London's domed St. Paul's Cathedral has an interesting architectural phenomenon called the "whispering gallery." One website explains it this way: "The name comes from the fact that a person who whispers facing the wall on one side can be clearly heard on the other, since the sound is carried perfectly around the vast curve of the Dome."

In other words, you and a friend could sit on opposite sides of architect Sir Christopher Wren's great cathedral and carry on a conversation without having to speak above a whisper.

While that may be a fascinating feature of St. Paul's Cathedral, it can also be a warning to us. What we say about others in secret can travel just as easily as whispers travel around that gallery. And not only can our gossip travel far and wide, but it often does great harm along the way.

Perhaps this is why the Bible frequently challenges us about the ways we use words. The wise King Solomon wrote, "In the multitude of words sin is not lacking, but he who restrains his lips is wise" (Proverbs 10:19 NKJV).

Instead of using whispers and gossip that can cause hurt and pain while serving no good purpose, we would do better to restrain ourselves and practice silence. 🌿

Where in your life do you feel drawn in to gossip or unnecessary conversation? How can you practice silence in those situations or remove yourself from them?

PROVERB

[*mashal*] (v. 1)

A proverb is a big idea housed in a tiny container. Through minimalist delivery, these brief sayings dazzle us with universal truth (applied to a particular context). The word for *proverb*, *mashal*, means "to compare, liken, be like." Proverbs often briefly compare one idea to another—set side by side, the truths radiate with life.

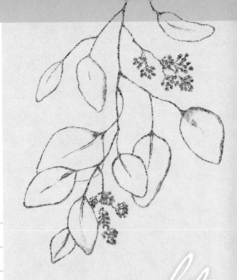

insight

ALL THE PROVERBS

Starting in chapter 10, we discover the profound one-liners that make Proverbs famous. Unlike the first nine chapters, you won't be hearing speeches about wisdom or folly. In fact, in chapters 10 through 30, you'll be hard-pressed to find an overarching theme. Instead, you'll be served pithy insight after pithy insight—chock-full of wisdom, literary power, and, at times, playful audacity—most of them written by the master of this art form, Solomon.

As you read chapter 10, what proverb attracts your attention?

Take time to listen to God's invitation for you through the proverb.

Proverbs 11

¹ *The Lord detests dishonest scales,*

but accurate weights find favor with him.

² When pride comes, then comes disgrace,
but with humility comes wisdom.

³ The integrity of the upright guides them,
but the unfaithful are destroyed by their duplicity.

⁴ Wealth is worthless in the day of wrath,
but righteousness delivers from death.

⁵ The righteousness of the blameless makes their
paths straight,
but the wicked are brought down by their own
wickedness.

⁶ The righteousness of the upright delivers them,
but the unfaithful are trapped by evil desires.

⁷ Hopes placed in mortals die with them;
  all the promise of their power comes to nothing.

⁸ The righteous person is rescued from trouble,
  and it falls on the wicked instead.

⁹ With their mouths the godless destroy their neighbors,
  but through knowledge the righteous escape.

¹⁰ When the righteous prosper, the city rejoices;
  when the wicked perish, there are shouts of joy.

¹¹ Through the blessing of the upright a city is exalted,
  but by the mouth of the wicked it is destroyed.

¹² Whoever derides their neighbor has no sense,
  but the one who has understanding holds their tongue.

¹³ A gossip betrays a confidence,
  but a trustworthy person keeps a secret.

¹⁴ For lack of guidance a nation falls,
  but victory is won through many advisers.

¹⁵ Whoever puts up security for a stranger will surely suffer,
  but whoever refuses to shake hands in pledge is safe.

¹⁶ A kindhearted woman gains honor,
  but ruthless men gain only wealth.

¹⁷ Those who are kind benefit themselves,
  but the cruel bring ruin on themselves.

¹⁸ A wicked person earns deceptive wages,
  but the one who sows righteousness reaps a sure reward.

¹⁹ Truly the righteous attain life,
  but whoever pursues evil finds death.

^{20} The LORD detests those whose hearts are perverse,
but he delights in those whose ways are blameless.

^{21} Be sure of this: The wicked will not go unpunished,
but those who are righteous will go free.

^{22} Like a gold ring in a pig's snout
is a beautiful woman who shows no discretion.

^{23} The desire of the righteous ends only in good,
but the hope of the wicked only in wrath.

^{24} One person gives freely, yet gains even more;
another withholds unduly, but comes to poverty.

^{25} A generous person will prosper;
whoever refreshes others will be refreshed.

²⁶ People curse the one who hoards grain,
    but they pray God's blessing on the one who is willing to sell.

²⁷ Whoever seeks good finds favor,
    but evil comes to one who searches for it.

²⁸ Those who trust in their riches will fall,
    but the righteous will thrive like a green leaf.

²⁹ Whoever brings ruin on their family will inherit only wind,
    and the fool will be servant to the wise.

³⁰ The fruit of the righteous is a tree of life,
    and the one who is wise saves lives.

³¹ If the righteous receive their due on earth,
    how much more the ungodly and the sinner! ❧

Sharing Slices

—KIRSTEN HOLMBERG

A generous person will prosper;
whoever refreshes others will be refreshed.

PROVERBS 11:25

Steve, a sixty-two-year-old homeless military veteran, made his way to a warm climate where sleeping outdoors was tolerable year round. One evening, as he displayed his hand-drawn art—his attempt to earn some money—a young woman approached and offered him several slices of pizza. Steve gratefully accepted. Moments later, Steve shared his bounty with another hungry, homeless person. Almost immediately, the same young woman resurfaced with another plate of food, acknowledging that he had been generous with what he'd been given.

Steve's story illustrates the principle found in Proverbs 11:25 that when we're generous with others, we're likely to experience generosity as well. But we shouldn't give with expecting something in return; rarely does our generosity return to us as quickly and obviously as it did for Steve. Rather, we give to help others in loving response to God's instruction to do so (Philippians 2:3–4; 1 John 3:17). And when we do, God is pleased. While he's under no obligation to refill our wallets or bellies, he often finds a way to refresh us—sometimes materially, other times spiritually.

Steve shared his second plate of pizza too with a smile and open hands. Despite his lack of resources, he is an example of what it means to live generously, willing to cheerfully share what we have with others instead of hoarding it for ourselves. As God leads and empowers us, may the same be said of us. 🍂

THE GENEROSITY OF WISDOM

A wise person is a generous one (11:25). In ancient Israel, to be considered *wise* (or its counterpart, *righteous*), you cared for the welfare of your community—particularly those who were vulnerable or marginalized (3:27–28). Proverbs 11:10 affirms, "When the righteous prosper, the city rejoices." That's because when the wise thrived, everyone else would too!

With whom can you share today?

How have you been blessed through another's generosity?

insight

LESSON IN PARALLELISM

Let's dive into Hebrew poetry: synonymous parallelism is simply when an idea repeats itself in more than one part of a proverb. For example, consider today's devotional verse: "A generous person will prosper; whoever refreshes others will be refreshed" (11:25). Here, the idea that *we're blessed by being generous* is stated twice—it just gets freshened up in the second part.

See if you can spot other examples of synonymous parallelism in chapter 11—if the two parts of a proverb are combined by the conjunction *and*, you've likely identified an example of synonymous parallelism (see v. 29).

Proverbs 12

¹ *Whoever loves discipline loves knowledge,*
> but whoever hates correction is stupid.

² Good people obtain favor from the LORD,
> but he condemns those who devise wicked schemes.

³ No one can be established through wickedness,
> but the righteous cannot be uprooted.

⁴ A wife of noble character is her husband's crown,
> but a disgraceful wife is like decay in his bones.

⁵ The plans of the righteous are just,
> but the advice of the wicked is deceitful.

⁶ The words of the wicked lie in wait for blood,
> but the speech of the upright rescues them.

⁷ The wicked are overthrown and are no more,
> but the house of the righteous stands firm.

⁸ A person is praised according to their
    prudence,
  and one with a warped mind is despised.

⁹ Better to be a nobody and yet have a servant
  than pretend to be somebody and have no
    food.

¹⁰ The righteous care for the needs of their
    animals,
  but the kindest acts of the wicked are
    cruel.

¹¹ Those who work their land will have
    abundant food,
  but those who chase fantasies have no
    sense.

¹² The wicked desire the stronghold of
    evildoers,
  but the root of the righteous endures.

¹³ Evildoers are trapped by their sinful talk,
  and so the innocent escape trouble.

¹⁴ From the fruit of their lips people are filled
    with good things,
  and the work of their hands brings them
    reward.

¹⁵ The way of fools seems right to them,
  but the wise listen to advice.

¹⁶ Fools show their annoyance at once,
  but the prudent overlook an insult.

¹⁷ An honest witness tells the truth,
  but a false witness tells lies.

¹⁸ The words of the reckless pierce like
    swords,
  but the tongue of the wise brings healing.

¹⁹ Truthful lips endure forever,
  but a lying tongue lasts only a moment.

²⁰ Deceit is in the hearts of those who plot
    evil,
  but those who promote peace have joy.

²¹ No harm overtakes the righteous,
  but the wicked have their fill of trouble.

²² The LORD detests lying lips,
  but he delights in people who are
    trustworthy.

²³ The prudent keep their knowledge to
    themselves,
  but a fool's heart blurts out folly.

²⁴ Diligent hands will rule,
  but laziness ends in forced labor.

²⁵ Anxiety weighs down the heart,
  but a kind word cheers it up.

²⁶ The righteous choose their friends carefully,
  but the way of the wicked leads them
    astray.

²⁷ The lazy do not roast any game,
  but the diligent feed on the riches of the
    hunt.

²⁸ In the way of righteousness there is life;
  along that path is immortality. 🌿

That Was Awesome!

—DAVE BRANON

Diligent hands will rule, but laziness ends in forced labor.

PROVERBS 12:24

It was the seventh grader's first cross-country meet, but she didn't want to run. Although she'd been preparing for the event, she was afraid of doing poorly. Still, she started the race with everyone else. Later, one by one the other runners finished the two-mile course and crossed the finish line—everyone except the reluctant runner. Finally, her mom, who was watching for her daughter to finish, saw a lone figure in the distance. The mother went to the finish line, preparing to comfort a distraught competitor. Instead, when the young runner saw her mom, she exclaimed, "That was awesome!"

What can be awesome about finishing last? Finishing!

The girl had tried something difficult and had accomplished it! Scripture honors hard work and diligence, a concept often learned through sports or music or other things that require perseverance and effort.

Proverbs 12:24 says, "Diligent hands will rule, but laziness ends in forced labor." And later we read, "All hard work brings a profit, but mere talk leads only to poverty" (14:23). These wise principles—not promises—can help us serve God well.

God's plan for us always included work. Even before the fall, Adam was to "work [the garden] and take care of it" (Genesis 2:15). And any effort we make should be done "with all [our] heart" (Colossians 3:23). Let's work in the strength he gives us—and leave the results to him. 🍃

HEIGHTENING THE DRAMA . . . THROUGH ANTITHETICAL PARALLELISM

We contrast things for dramatic effect. In his proverbs, Solomon creates tension through contrast. Consider today's devotional verse: "Diligent hands will rule, but laziness ends in forced labor" (12:24). Solomon could have simply said, *Be diligent*—but consider the voltage of his words contrasting the results of hard work and laziness!

This is an example of antithetical parallelism—the literary device that adds drama by highlighting differences. See if you can find one of the twenty-two examples of antithetical parallelism in chapter 12 (you've spotted antithetical parallelism when a proverb is joined by the word *but*).

insight

What are some areas where I can learn from this teenager to be diligent and persevere?

How does doing my best and working hard honor God?

Proverbs 13

¹ *A wise son heeds his father's instruction,*
but a mocker does not respond to rebukes.

² From the fruit of their lips people enjoy good things,
but the unfaithful have an appetite for violence.

³ Those who guard their lips preserve their lives,
but those who speak rashly will come to ruin.

⁴ A sluggard's appetite is never filled,
but the desires of the diligent are fully satisfied.

⁵ The righteous hate what is false,
but the wicked make themselves a stench
and bring shame on themselves.

⁶ Righteousness guards the person of integrity,
but wickedness overthrows the sinner.

7 One person pretends to be rich, yet has
   nothing;
 another pretends to be poor, yet has great
   wealth.

8 A person's riches may ransom their life,
   but the poor cannot respond to threatening
   rebukes.

9 The light of the righteous shines brightly,
   but the lamp of the wicked is snuffed out.

10 Where there is strife, there is pride,
   but wisdom is found in those who take
   advice.

11 Dishonest money dwindles away,
   but whoever gathers money little by little
   makes it grow.

12 Hope deferred makes the heart sick,
   but a longing fulfilled is a tree of life.

13 Whoever scorns instruction will pay for it,
   but whoever respects a command is
   rewarded.

14 The teaching of the wise is a fountain of life,
   turning a person from the snares of death.

15 Good judgment wins favor,
   but the way of the unfaithful leads to their
   destruction.

16 All who are prudent act with knowledge,
   but fools expose their folly.

17 A wicked messenger falls into trouble,
   but a trustworthy envoy brings healing.

18 Whoever disregards discipline comes to
   poverty and shame,
   but whoever heeds correction is honored.

19 A longing fulfilled is sweet to the soul,
   but fools detest turning from evil.

20 Walk with the wise and become wise,
   for a companion of fools suffers harm.

21 Trouble pursues the sinner,
   but the righteous are rewarded with good
   things.

22 A good person leaves an inheritance for
   their children's children,
   but a sinner's wealth is stored up for the
   righteous.

23 An unplowed field produces food for the
   poor,
   but injustice sweeps it away.

24 Whoever spares the rod hates their children,
   but the one who loves their children is
   careful to discipline them.

25 The righteous eat to their hearts' content,
   but the stomach of the wicked goes
   hungry. 🌿

The Two Bears

—DAVID H. ROPER

Where there is strife, there is pride,
but wisdom is found in those who take advice.

PROVERBS 13:10

Who in your circle of friends welcomes constructive feedback?

How does the need to be right lead to conflict?

As you read chapter 13, what proverb attracts your attention? Take time to listen to God's invitation for you through the proverb.

Some years ago, my wife, Carolyn, and I spent a few days camping on the flanks of Mount Rainier in Washington State. When we were returning to our campsite one evening, we saw in the middle of a meadow two male bears boxing each other's ears. We stopped to watch.

There was a hiker nearby, and I asked him what the conflict was about. "A young female," he said.

"Where is she?" I asked.

"Oh, she left about twenty minutes ago," he chuckled. Thus, I gathered, the conflict at this point was not about the female bear but about being the toughest bear.

Most fights aren't about policy and principle, or about right and wrong; they're almost always about pride. The wise man of Proverbs swings his axe at the root of the problem when he writes: "Pride leads to conflict" (13:10 NLT). Quarrels are fueled by pride, by needing to be right, by wanting our way, or by defending our turf or our egos.

On the other side, wisdom resides with the well-advised—those who listen and learn, those who allow themselves to be instructed. There is wisdom in those who humble themselves—those who set aside their own selfish ambition, who acknowledge the limits of their own understanding, who listen to the other person's point of view, who allow their own ideas to be corrected. This is the wisdom from God that spreads peace wherever it goes.

PRIDE

[zadon] (v. 10)
To live with pride
(*zadon* in Hebrew), according to the book of Proverbs,
is to live in rebellion against the divine wisdom that God
has built into the universe. The nature of reality is such
that to live well requires us to have a deep awe or
"fear" of God (Proverbs 9:10). To resist living with
humility and awe before God—to live with pride—is
profoundly foolish, as it runs contrary to the grain
of reality and can only cause suffering and harm.
Lady Wisdom, on the other hand, "is a tree of life to
those who take hold of her" (Proverbs 3:18).

ALL ABOUT WISDOM— PROVERBS, ECCLESIASTES, AND JOB

In the Bible, three books—Proverbs, Ecclesiastes, and Job—are identified as *Wisdom Literature*. Each focuses on cultivating *wisdom* (Hebrew *chokmah*), which can be defined as living well, that is, living in tune with God's wisdom woven into the fabric of the universe.

As you read biblical Wisdom Literature, it's helpful to keep a few principles in mind. First, Proverbs, Ecclesiastics, and Job are each equally important works of Wisdom Literature designed to complement—not compete with—each other. In this context, Proverbs is the beginner's guide to wisdom, providing general principles that reflect God's designs for the universe. Although living in tune with these principles is more likely to lead to a flourishing life than living foolishly, the verses in Proverbs are *not* intended to be promises that eliminate exceptions. That is, God hasn't broken a promise if, despite a life of wisdom, your dreams are thwarted and you endure great suffering (Proverbs 10:24–28), die before you reach old age (10:27), or your children wander from wisdom (22:6).

The books of Job and Ecclesiastes both wrestle with the troubling question of how to respond within experiences of suffering and injustice we are powerless to prevent. By including each of these books of Wisdom Literature in the Bible, we're given a holistic view of life's complexity, one that requires us to continually draw closer to God for healing and growth in wisdom.

Proverbs 14

¹ *The wise woman builds her house,*
  but with her own hands the foolish one tears hers down.

² Whoever fears the Lord walks uprightly,
  but those who despise him are devious in their ways.

³ A fool's mouth lashes out with pride,
  but the lips of the wise protect them.

⁴ Where there are no oxen, the manger is empty,
  but from the strength of an ox come abundant harvests.

⁵ An honest witness does not deceive,
  but a false witness pours out lies.

⁶ The mocker seeks wisdom and finds none,
  but knowledge comes easily to the discerning.

⁷ Stay away from a fool,
  for you will not find knowledge on their lips.

⁸ The wisdom of the prudent is to give thought to their ways,
  but the folly of fools is deception.

⁹ Fools mock at making amends for sin,
  but goodwill is found among the upright.

¹⁰ Each heart knows its own bitterness,
  and no one else can share its joy.

¹¹ The house of the wicked will be destroyed,
  but the tent of the upright will flourish.

¹² There is a way that appears to be right,
  but in the end it leads to death.

¹³ Even in laughter the heart may ache,
  and rejoicing may end in grief.

¹⁴ The faithless will be fully repaid for their ways,
  and the good rewarded for theirs.

¹⁵ The simple believe anything,
  but the prudent give thought to their steps.

¹⁶ The wise fear the Lord and shun evil,
  but a fool is hotheaded and yet feels secure.

¹⁷ A quick-tempered person does foolish things,
  and the one who devises evil schemes is hated.

¹⁸ The simple inherit folly,
  but the prudent are crowned with knowledge.

¹⁹ Evildoers will bow down in the presence of the good,
  and the wicked at the gates of the righteous.

²⁰ The poor are shunned even by their neighbors,
   but the rich have many friends.

²¹ It is a sin to despise one's neighbor,
   but blessed is the one who is kind to the needy.

²² Do not those who plot evil go astray?
   But those who plan what is good find love and faithfulness.

²³ All hard work brings a profit,
   but mere talk leads only to poverty.

²⁴ The wealth of the wise is their crown,
   but the folly of fools yields folly.

²⁵ A truthful witness saves lives,
   but a false witness is deceitful.

²⁶ Whoever fears the LORD has a secure fortress,
   and for their children it will be a refuge.

²⁷ The fear of the LORD is a fountain of life,
   turning a person from the snares of death.

²⁸ A large population is a king's glory,
  but without subjects a prince is ruined.

²⁹ Whoever is patient has great understanding,
  but one who is quick-tempered displays folly.

³⁰ A heart at peace gives life to the body,
  but envy rots the bones.

³¹ Whoever oppresses the poor shows contempt for their Maker,
  but whoever is kind to the needy honors God.

³² When calamity comes, the wicked are brought down,
  but even in death the righteous seek refuge in God.

³³ Wisdom reposes in the heart of the discerning
  and even among fools she lets herself be known.

³⁴ Righteousness exalts a nation,
  but sin condemns any people.

³⁵ A king delights in a wise servant,
  but a shameful servant arouses his fury. ❧

A Wise Builder

—LINDA WASHINGTON

The wise woman builds her house,
but with her own hands the foolish one tears hers down.

PROVERBS 14:1

Sojourner Truth, whose birth name was Isabella Baumfree, was born a slave in 1797 in Esopus, New York. Though nearly all of her children were sold as slaves, she escaped to freedom in 1826 with one daughter and lived with a family who paid the money for her freedom. Instead of allowing an unjust system to keep her family apart, she took legal action to regain her small son Peter—an amazing feat for an African-American woman in that day. Knowing she couldn't raise her children without God's help, she became a believer in Christ and later changed her name to Sojourner Truth to show that her life was built on the foundation of God's truth.

King Solomon, the writer of Proverbs 14:1, declares, "The wise woman builds her house." In contrast, one without wisdom "tears hers down." This building metaphor shows the wisdom God provides to those willing to listen. How does one build a house with wisdom? By saying "only what is helpful for building others up" (Ephesians 4:29; see also 1 Thessalonians 5:11). How does one tear down? Proverbs 14 gives the answer: "A fool's mouth lashes out with pride" (v. 3).

Sojourner had a "secure fortress" (v. 26) in a turbulent time, thanks to the wisdom of God. You may never have to rescue your children from an injustice. But you can build your house on the same foundation Sojourner did—the wisdom of God. 🐌

IN HER OWN WORDS: SOJOURNER TRUTH

Today's devotional features Sojourner Truth, a fearless abolitionist and women's activist. In 1863, Sojourner courageously led an abolition movement in Indiana—after the state barred African Americans from setting foot inside it. For staying in the state, she was jailed twice. Undeterred, Sojourner continued her abolition sessions upon her release. Her friends, afraid for her safety because she'd received death threats, recommended she carry a gun. Undaunted, Sojourner replied, "I carry no weapon; the Lord will [preserve] me without weapons. I feel safe in the midst of my enemies; for the truth is powerful and will prevail."*

---

* Olive Gilbert and Frances W. Titus, *Sojourner Truth's Narrative and Book of Life* (Battle Creek, MI: published for the author, 1878), https://www.loc.gov/item/29025244/.

What foundation is your house established upon?

How will you build your house this week?

—PRAY—

Jesus, thank you for the illustration of the wise woman in Proverbs 14:1, who with the strength of her will, mind, and hands built a house that stood firm. Help me build my home—that is my life and everything and everyone it touches—in wisdom and power today.

As I build my house, I ask for the grit to stick with my work and to respond in love to others. I'm not perfect, and I will fail again and again—but give me the courage and tenacity to get back up and try again. Give me patience, both with those around me and with myself, in my interactions today. Finally, I ask for ingenuity to solve problems, bring ideas to life, and discern my path. I am so thankful to have the God of the universe on my side as I press on each day.

I love you. Thank you for being the safe and secure foundation of my home.

In Jesus's name, Amen.

Proverbs 15

¹ *A gentle answer turns away wrath,*
> but a harsh word stirs up anger.

² The tongue of the wise adorns knowledge,
> but the mouth of the fool gushes folly.

³ The eyes of the LORD are everywhere,
> keeping watch on the wicked and the good.

⁴ The soothing tongue is a tree of life,
> but a perverse tongue crushes the spirit.

⁵ A fool spurns a parent's discipline,
> but whoever heeds correction shows prudence.

⁶ The house of the righteous contains great treasure,
> but the income of the wicked brings ruin.

⁷ The lips of the wise spread knowledge,
> but the hearts of fools are not upright.

⁸ The LORD detests the sacrifice of the wicked,
   but the prayer of the upright pleases him.

⁹ The LORD detests the way of the wicked,
   but he loves those who pursue righteousness.

¹⁰ Stern discipline awaits anyone who leaves the path;
   the one who hates correction will die.

¹¹ Death and Destruction lie open before the LORD—
   how much more do human hearts!

¹² Mockers resent correction,
   so they avoid the wise.

¹³ A happy heart makes the face cheerful,
   but heartache crushes the spirit.

¹⁴ The discerning heart seeks knowledge,
   but the mouth of a fool feeds on folly.

¹⁵ All the days of the oppressed are wretched,
   but the cheerful heart has a continual feast.

¹⁶ Better a little with the fear of the LORD
   than great wealth with turmoil.

¹⁷ Better a small serving of vegetables with love
   than a fattened calf with hatred.

¹⁸ A hot-tempered person stirs up conflict,
   but the one who is patient calms a quarrel.

¹⁹ The way of the sluggard is blocked with thorns,
   but the path of the upright is a highway.

²⁰ A wise son brings joy to his father,
   but a foolish man despises his mother.

²¹ Folly brings joy to one who has no sense,
    but whoever has understanding keeps a straight course.

²² Plans fail for lack of counsel,
    but with many advisers they succeed.

²³ A person finds joy in giving an apt reply—
    and how good is a timely word!

²⁴ The path of life leads upward for the prudent
    to keep them from going down to the realm of the dead.

²⁵ The LORD tears down the house of the proud,
    but he sets the widow's boundary stones in place.

²⁶ The LORD detests the thoughts of the wicked,
    but gracious words are pure in his sight.

²⁷ The greedy bring ruin to their households,
    but the one who hates bribes will live.

²⁸ The heart of the righteous weighs its answers,
    but the mouth of the wicked gushes evil.

²⁹ The LORD is far from the wicked,
    but he hears the prayer of the righteous.

³⁰ Light in a messenger's eyes brings joy to the heart,
    and good news gives health to the bones.

³¹ Whoever heeds life-giving correction
    will be at home among the wise.

³² Those who disregard discipline despise themselves,
    but the one who heeds correction gains understanding.

³³ Wisdom's instruction is to fear the LORD,
    and humility comes before honor. ❧

A Critical Reaction

—PATRICIA RAYBON

The one who is patient calms a quarrel.

PROVERBS 15:18

Tough words hurt. So my friend—an award-winning author—struggled with how to respond to the criticism he received. His new book had earned five-star reviews plus a major award. Then a respected magazine reviewer gave him a backhanded compliment, describing his book as well-written yet still criticizing it harshly. Turning to friends, he asked, "How should I reply?"

One friend advised, "Let it go." I shared advice from writing magazines, including tips to ignore such criticism or learn from it even while continuing to work and write.

Finally, however, I decided to see what Scripture—which has the best advice of all—has to say about how to react to strong criticism. The book of James advises, "Everyone should be quick to listen, slow to speak and slow to become angry" (1:19). The apostle Paul counsels us to "live in harmony with one another" (Romans 12:16).

An entire chapter of Proverbs, however, offers extended wisdom on reacting to disputes. "A gentle answer turns away wrath," says Proverbs 15:1. "The one who is patient calms a quarrel" (v. 18). Also, "the one who heeds correction gains understanding" (v. 32). Considering such wisdom, may God help us hold our tongues, as my friend did. More than all, however, wisdom instructs us to "fear the LORD" because "humility comes before honor" (v. 33). 🐚

HUMILITY

[anah] (v. 33)
Humility unlocks the treasures of wisdom, according to Proverbs (11:2; 22:4). The word for *humility* originates in the Hebrew root *anah*, "to be afflicted, bowed down" or "to be humbled or meek." Throughout Proverbs, we're talking about that second definition (see the related concept in chapter 9: Fear). Someone with humility listens to God. They also learn from their mistakes, from God, and from those around them. Through humility, we gain wisdom—often along with honor, success, and purpose (15:33; 18:12; 22:4).

Humility is contrasted to pride in Proverbs: "Before a downfall the heart is haughty, but humility comes before honor" (18:12). Unlike humility, pride is the antithesis of wisdom and leads to devastation (16:18).

What's your typical reaction when you're criticized?

In a dispute, what's a humble way you can guard your tongue?

insight

IDENTIFYING BETTER-THAN PARALLELISM

The proverbs that start with "better" help us discern between a wise and an unwise path. For example, in chapter 15, Proverbs says, "*Better* a small serving of vegetables with love than a fattened calf with hatred" (v. 17, italics added). The poem compares two home environments—a happy family of limited means and a wealthy, unhappy home. Through the comparison, we discover that being relatively poor yet happy is the wiser lifestyle. This form of Hebrew poetry is better-than parallelism.

Proverbs 16

¹ *To humans belong the plans of the heart,*

but from the LORD comes the proper answer of the tongue.

² All a person's ways seem pure to them,
   but motives are weighed by the LORD.

³ Commit to the LORD whatever you do,
   and he will establish your plans.

⁴ The LORD works out everything to its proper end—
   even the wicked for a day of disaster.

⁵ The LORD detests all the proud of heart.
   Be sure of this: They will not go unpunished.

⁶ Through love and faithfulness sin is atoned for;
   through the fear of the LORD evil is avoided.

⁷ When the LORD takes pleasure in anyone's way,
   he causes their enemies to make peace with them.

⁸ Better a little with righteousness
  than much gain with injustice.

⁹ In their hearts humans plan their course,
  but the Lᴏʀᴅ establishes their steps.

¹⁰ The lips of a king speak as an oracle,
  and his mouth does not betray justice.

¹¹ Honest scales and balances belong to the Lᴏʀᴅ;
  all the weights in the bag are of his making.

¹² Kings detest wrongdoing,
  for a throne is established through righteousness.

¹³ Kings take pleasure in honest lips;
  they value the one who speaks what is right.

¹⁴ A king's wrath is a messenger of death,
  but the wise will appease it.

¹⁵ When a king's face brightens, it means life;
  his favor is like a rain cloud in spring.

¹⁶ How much better to get wisdom than gold,
  to get insight rather than silver!

¹⁷ The highway of the upright avoids evil;
  those who guard their ways preserve their lives.

¹⁸ Pride goes before destruction,
  a haughty spirit before a fall.

¹⁹ Better to be lowly in spirit along with the oppressed
than to share plunder with the proud.

²⁰ Whoever gives heed to instruction prospers,
and blessed is the one who trusts in the LORD.

²¹ The wise in heart are called discerning,
and gracious words promote instruction.

²² Prudence is a fountain of life to the prudent,
but folly brings punishment to fools.

²³ The hearts of the wise make their mouths prudent,
and their lips promote instruction.

²⁴ Gracious words are a honeycomb,
sweet to the soul and healing to the bones.

²⁵ There is a way that appears to be right,
but in the end it leads to death.

²⁶ The appetite of laborers works for them;
   their hunger drives them on.

²⁷ A scoundrel plots evil,
   and on their lips it is like a scorching fire.

²⁸ A perverse person stirs up conflict,
   and a gossip separates close friends.

²⁹ A violent person entices their neighbor
   and leads them down a path that is not good.

³⁰ Whoever winks with their eye is plotting perversity;
   whoever purses their lips is bent on evil.

³¹ Gray hair is a crown of splendor;
   it is attained in the way of righteousness.

³² Better a patient person than a warrior,
   one with self-control than one who takes a city.

³³ The lot is cast into the lap,
   but its every decision is from the Lord. ❧

Whatever We Do

—XOCHITL DIXON

Commit to the LORD whatever you do,
and he will establish your plans.

PROVERBS 16:3

In *Surprised by Joy*, C. S. Lewis confessed he came to Christianity at the age of thirty-three, "kicking, struggling, resentful, and darting his eyes in every direction for a chance to escape." Despite Lewis's own personal resistance, his shortcomings, and the obstacles he faced, the Lord transformed him into a courageous and creative defender of the faith. Lewis proclaimed God's truth and love through writing powerful essays and novels that are still being read, studied, and shared more than fifty-five years after his death. His life reflected the belief that a person is never too old to set another goal or dream a new dream.

As we make plans and follow dreams, God can purify our motives and empower us to devote whatever we do to him (Proverbs 16:1–3). From the most ordinary tasks to the greatest challenges, we can live for the glory of our almighty Maker, who "works out everything to its proper end" (v. 4). Every action, every word, and every thought can become an expression of heartfelt worship, a sacrificial gift to honor our Lord, as he watches over us (v. 7).

God can't be limited by our limitations, our reservations, or our tendencies to settle or dream small. As we choose to live for him—dedicated to and dependent on him—he will bring about his plans for us. Whatever we do can be done with him, for him, and only because of him. 🌿

What steps can you take to honor God as you follow a dream he's placed on your heart?

What dreams, plans, or burdens do you need to commit to Jesus today (16:3)?

Talk with him about them.

THE FRUIT OF DISCERNMENT

Do you second-guess your choices? Instead of worrying, observe the fruit of your decisions. The apostle Paul says we grow the fruit of the Spirit—love, joy, peace, forbearance, kindness, goodness, faithfulness, gentleness and self-control—when we follow him (Galatians 5:22–23). After making a God-honoring choice, these fruits should be evident! So, for example, are you experiencing an increasing sense of peace following your decision? Are you growing in your love for others and for God? Have you become more joyful because of your choice? These are likely signs that your decision is bearing good fruit.

COMMIT

[*galal*] (v. 3)

Today's key verse, 16:3, says to "commit" our plans to God. The word *commit*—*galal*—literally means "to roll" or "to roll away." In the Old Testament, including later in Proverbs, the word describes rolling away boulders (26:27; Genesis 29:3, 8, 10). Through *galal*, we receive a powerful invitation—a call to roll our heavy loads onto Jesus! The same encouragement is offered in Psalm 37:5: "Commit [roll] your way to the LORD; trust in him." Jesus longs for us to let go of our dreams, anxieties, and plans—and roll them onto him.

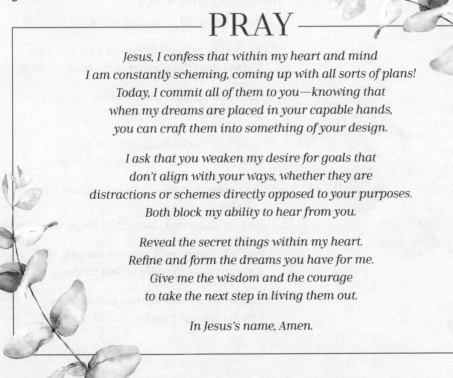

PRAY

*Jesus, I confess that within my heart and mind
I am constantly scheming, coming up with all sorts of plans!
Today, I commit all of them to you—knowing that
when my dreams are placed in your capable hands,
you can craft them into something of your design.*

*I ask that you weaken my desire for goals that
don't align with your ways, whether they are
distractions or schemes directly opposed to your purposes.
Both block my ability to hear from you.*

*Reveal the secret things within my heart.
Refine and form the dreams you have for me.
Give me the wisdom and the courage
to take the next step in living them out.*

In Jesus's name, Amen.

Proverbs 17

¹ *Better a dry crust with peace and quiet*
   than a house full of feasting, with strife.

² A prudent servant will rule over a disgraceful son
   and will share the inheritance as one of the family.

³ The crucible for silver and the furnace for gold,
   but the LORD tests the heart.

⁴ A wicked person listens to deceitful lips;
   a liar pays attention to a destructive tongue.

⁵ Whoever mocks the poor shows contempt for their
      Maker;
   whoever gloats over disaster will not go unpunished.

⁶ Children's children are a crown to the aged,
   and parents are the pride of their children.

⁷ Eloquent lips are unsuited to a godless fool—
   how much worse lying lips to a ruler!

⁸ A bribe is seen as a charm by the one who
  gives it;
  they think success will come at every turn.

⁹ Whoever would foster love covers over an
  offense,
  but whoever repeats the matter separates
  close friends.

¹⁰ A rebuke impresses a discerning person
  more than a hundred lashes a fool.

¹¹ Evildoers foster rebellion against God;
  the messenger of death will be sent against
  them.

¹² Better to meet a bear robbed of her cubs
  than a fool bent on folly.

¹³ Evil will never leave the house
  of one who pays back evil for good.

¹⁴ Starting a quarrel is like breaching a dam;
  so drop the matter before a dispute breaks
  out.

¹⁵ Acquitting the guilty and condemning the
  innocent—
  the Lord detests them both.

¹⁶ Why should fools have money in hand to buy
  wisdom,
  when they are not able to understand it?

¹⁷ A friend loves at all times,
  and a brother is born for a time of adversity.

¹⁸ One who has no sense shakes hands in pledge
  and puts up security for a neighbor.

¹⁹ Whoever loves a quarrel loves sin;
  whoever builds a high gate invites destruction.

²⁰ One whose heart is corrupt does not prosper;
  one whose tongue is perverse falls into
  trouble.

²¹ To have a fool for a child brings grief;
  there is no joy for the parent of a godless fool.

²² A cheerful heart is good medicine,
  but a crushed spirit dries up the bones.

²³ The wicked accept bribes in secret
  to pervert the course of justice.

²⁴ A discerning person keeps wisdom in view,
  but a fool's eyes wander to the ends of the
  earth.

²⁵ A foolish son brings grief to his father
  and bitterness to the mother who bore him.

²⁶ If imposing a fine on the innocent is not good,
  surely to flog honest officials is not right.

²⁷ The one who has knowledge uses words with
  restraint,
  and whoever has understanding is even-
  tempered.

²⁸ Even fools are thought wise if they keep silent,
  and discerning if they hold their tongues. ❧

Biblical Prescription

—LISA M. SAMRA

A cheerful heart is good medicine,
but a crushed spirit dries up the bones.

PROVERBS 17:22

Greg and Elizabeth have a regular "Joke Night" with their four school-age children. Each child brings several jokes they've read or heard (or made up themselves!) during the week to tell at the dinner table. This tradition has created joyful memories of fun shared around the table. Greg and Elizabeth even noticed the laughter was healthy for their children, lifting their spirits on difficult days.

The benefit of joyful conversation around the dinner table was observed by C. S. Lewis, who wrote, "The sun looks down on nothing half so good as a household laughing together over a meal."

The wisdom of fostering a joyful heart is found in Proverbs 17:22, where we read, "A cheerful heart is good medicine, but a crushed spirit dries up the bones." The proverb offers a "prescription" to stimulate health and healing—allowing joy to fill our hearts, a medicine that costs little and yields great results.

We all need this biblical prescription. When we bring joy into our conversations, it can put a disagreement into perspective. It can help us to experience peace, even after a stressful test at school or a difficult day at work. Laughter among family and friends can create a safe place where we both know and feel that we're loved.

Do you need to incorporate more laughter into your life as "good medicine" for your spirit? Remember, you have encouragement from Scripture to cultivate a cheerful heart. 🕮

EXPLORING HEBREW POETRY

Solomon furnishes his proverbs with images from every-day life: a "house full of feasting" (17:1), "honeycomb" (16:24), a "rushing stream" (18:4), and "deep waters" (18:4). Such word pictures are strategic; Solomon fastens a familiar image to a less-familiar idea (usually the key takeaway) to illuminate the truth.

For example, consider Proverbs 17:12: "Better to meet a bear robbed of her cubs than a fool bent on folly." Through the image of the enraged mother bear, we immediately recognize the proverb's point—*entangling yourself in the schemes of a fool is deadly*. See if you can find other images that unlock the truth of the proverb.

PROVERBS IN THE NEW TESTAMENT?

insight

The word for *proverb* in Hebrew (*mashal*) is translated to "parable" (*parabole*) in New Testament Greek. Thus, Jesus, who educated through parables, was a master of the proverb! Jesus even self-identified as a wisdom teacher by comparing himself with Solomon (Matthew 12:42).

How has good humor helped you deal with life's challenges recently?

What does it mean for you to be filled with the joy of the Lord?

As you read chapter 17, which proverb attracts your attention? Take time to listen to God's invitation for you through the proverb.

Proverbs 18

^{1}*An unfriendly person pursues selfish ends*
and against all sound judgment starts quarrels.

^{2}Fools find no pleasure in understanding
but delight in airing their own opinions.

^{3}When wickedness comes, so does contempt,
and with shame comes reproach.

^{4}The words of the mouth are deep waters,
but the fountain of wisdom is a rushing stream.

^{5}It is not good to be partial to the wicked
and so deprive the innocent of justice.

^{6}The lips of fools bring them strife,
and their mouths invite a beating.

^{7}The mouths of fools are their undoing,
and their lips are a snare to their very lives.

⁸ The words of a gossip are like choice morsels;
  they go down to the inmost parts.

⁹ One who is slack in his work
  is brother to one who destroys.

¹⁰ The name of the LORD is a fortified tower;
  the righteous run to it and are safe.

¹¹ The wealth of the rich is their fortified city;
  they imagine it a wall too high to scale.

¹² Before a downfall the heart is haughty,
  but humility comes before honor.

¹³ To answer before listening—
  that is folly and shame.

¹⁴ The human spirit can endure in sickness,
  but a crushed spirit who can bear?

¹⁵ The heart of the discerning acquires knowledge,
  for the ears of the wise seek it out.

¹⁶ A gift opens the way
  and ushers the giver into the presence of
  the great.

¹⁷ In a lawsuit the first to speak seems right,
  until someone comes forward and
  cross-examines.

¹⁸ Casting the lot settles disputes
  and keeps strong opponents apart.

¹⁹ A brother wronged is more unyielding than
  a fortified city;
  disputes are like the barred gates of a
  citadel.

²⁰ From the fruit of their mouth a person's
  stomach is filled;
  with the harvest of their lips they are
  satisfied.

²¹ The tongue has the power of life and death,
  and those who love it will eat its fruit.

²² He who finds a wife finds what is good
  and receives favor from the LORD.

²³ The poor plead for mercy,
  but the rich answer harshly.

²⁴ One who has unreliable friends soon comes
  to ruin,
  but there is a friend who sticks closer than
  a brother.

The Power of Words

—MARVIN WILLIAMS

Death and life are in the power of the tongue,
and those who love it will eat its fruit.

PROVERBS 18:21 (NRSV)

Nelson Mandela, who opposed the South African apartheid regime and was imprisoned for almost three decades, knew the power of words. He is often quoted today, but while in prison his words could not be quoted for fear of repercussion. A decade after his release he said, "It is never my custom to use words lightly. If twenty-seven years in prison have done anything to us, it was to use the silence of solitude to make us understand how precious words are, and how real speech is in its impact on the way people live and die."

King Solomon, author of most of the Old Testament book of Proverbs, wrote often about the power of words. He said, "Death and life are in the power of the tongue" (Proverbs 18:21 NRSV). Words have the potential to produce positive or negative consequences (v. 20). They have the power to give life through encouragement and honesty or to crush and kill through lies and gossip. How can we be assured of producing good words that have a positive outcome? The only way is by diligently guarding our hearts: "Above all else, guard your heart, for everything you do flows from it" (4:23).

Jesus can transform our hearts so that our words can truly be their best—honest, calm, appropriate, and suitable for the situation. 🕊

Who has spoken life-giving words to you? What about their words renewed your spirit?

In what ways do you desire God's healing or transformation within your heart right now?
    Take time to talk with Jesus about it.

Thinking about Nelson Mandela's quote in today's devotional, do you ever "use words lightly"? In what way do they have "impact on the way people live and die"?

SPEAKING WITH WISDOM

insight

Proverbs calls us to take our use of language seriously. (Read James 3 for similar admonitions.) In a sense, our words are a primary demonstration of whether we have chosen the path of folly or wisdom. With our words, we can either bless others with God's divine, life-giving wisdom, or we can harm them with the opposite, the "death" that stems from foolishness (Proverbs 18:21). To speak foolishly, then, is a grievous moral failing—as it reflects allegiance to Lady Folly instead of Woman Wisdom, a heart and lifestyle choice that can only cause ourselves and others great pain.

— PRAY —

Jesus, my words overflow from what lies within my heart, and sometimes that's an alarming thought! Please tend to and cultivate my heart (Psalm 51). Weed out the evil sometimes rooted there, whether envy, bitterness, pride, lust, or self-absorption, and grow the fruit of the Spirit in me, your peace, patience, kindness, joy, and love (Galatians 5:22–23).

I also ask for discernment in what I say. Give me life-giving speech, fill my words with power and love, and free me to speak and to refrain from speaking at the appropriate times.

In Jesus's name, Amen.

Proverbs 19

¹ *Better the poor whose walk is blameless*
  than a fool whose lips are perverse.

² Desire without knowledge is not good—
    how much more will hasty feet miss the way!

³ A person's own folly leads to their ruin,
    yet their heart rages against the LORD.

⁴ Wealth attracts many friends,
    but even the closest friend of the poor person
      deserts them.

⁵ A false witness will not go unpunished,
    and whoever pours out lies will not go free.

⁶ Many curry favor with a ruler,
    and everyone is the friend of one who gives gifts.

⁷ The poor are shunned by all their relatives—
    how much more do their friends avoid them!
  Though the poor pursue them with pleading,
    they are nowhere to be found.

⁸ The one who gets wisdom loves life;
   the one who cherishes understanding will
      soon prosper.

⁹ A false witness will not go unpunished,
   and whoever pours out lies will perish.

¹⁰ It is not fitting for a fool to live in luxury—
   how much worse for a slave to rule over
      princes!

¹¹ A person's wisdom yields patience;
   it is to one's glory to overlook an offense.

¹² A king's rage is like the roar of a lion,
   but his favor is like dew on the grass.

¹³ A foolish child is a father's ruin,
   and a quarrelsome wife is like
      the constant dripping of a leaky roof.

¹⁴ Houses and wealth are inherited from
      parents,
   but a prudent wife is from the LORD.

¹⁵ Laziness brings on deep sleep,
   and the shiftless go hungry.

¹⁶ Whoever keeps commandments keeps their
      life,
   but whoever shows contempt for their ways
      will die.

¹⁷ Whoever is kind to the poor lends to the
      LORD,
   and he will reward them for what they have
      done.

¹⁸ Discipline your children, for in that there is
      hope;
   do not be a willing party to their death.

¹⁹ A hot-tempered person must pay the penalty;
   rescue them, and you will have to do it
      again.

²⁰ Listen to advice and accept discipline,
   and at the end you will be counted among
      the wise.

²¹ Many are the plans in a person's heart,
   but it is the LORD's purpose that prevails.

²² What a person desires is unfailing love;
   better to be poor than a liar.

²³ The fear of the LORD leads to life;
   then one rests content, untouched by
      trouble.

²⁴ A sluggard buries his hand in the dish;
   he will not even bring it back to his mouth!

²⁵ Flog a mocker, and the simple will learn
      prudence;
   rebuke the discerning, and they will gain
      knowledge.

²⁶ Whoever robs their father and drives out
      their mother
   is a child who brings shame and disgrace.

²⁷ Stop listening to instruction, my son,
   and you will stray from the words of
      knowledge.

²⁸ A corrupt witness mocks at justice,
   and the mouth of the wicked gulps down
      evil.

²⁹ Penalties are prepared for mockers,
   and beatings for the backs of fools. ❧

What's At Stake?

—ANNE CETAS

Listen to counsel and receive instruction, that you may be wise in your latter days.

PROVERBS 19:20 (NKJV)

To stake or not to stake? That's the question Marilyn faced when she planted a tree sapling last summer. The salesman said, "Stake it for one year so it will be supported in strong winds. Then remove them so it can grow deep roots on its own." But a neighbor told her, "Staking may cause more harm than good. The tree needs to start building strong roots right away, or it may never. Not staking is best for long-term health."

We wonder about that question in relationships too. For instance, if someone has gotten himself into trouble, do we "stake him down" by rescuing him, or do we let the person "grow strong roots" on his own by allowing him to face the consequences of his choices? Obviously, it depends on what seems best for the person's long-term spiritual health. What does love do, and when does it do it? Proverbs 19 gives opposite thoughts: We are to be "kind" and lend our assistance (v. 17), yet there are dangers in rescuing another because you might need to do it again (v. 19). Providing the right help requires wisdom beyond our own.

God hasn't left us on our own. He will give us the wisdom when we ask him. And as we lean on him, our own roots will grow deep in him as well. 🌱

How is God leading you to help someone in this season? Talk with Jesus about it.

How is God leading you to set healthy boundaries in your relationships?

LISTEN

[shama] (v. 20)

When children hear a stern, exasperated "Listen to me!" from their parents, they know that they are not only to *listen with their ears* but *also to obey whatever their parents say next.* The word *listen* in Hebrew, *shama*, contains a similar idea. *Shama* can be translated *hear, listen, pay attention to, perceive, obey, proclaim,* or *announce. Listen* or *hear* can often be exchanged with *obey* in the Old Testament—as is the case in today's devotional verse (19:20) and throughout much of Proverbs. That's because obedience is the bedrock of wisdom, according to the authors of Proverbs (1:8; 10:17; 29:23). To become wise, we must first *listen* to instruction from God and others and then *obey* it by humbly integrating their guidance into our lives.

LISTENING TO GOD'S VOICE

insight

How do we discern God's ways amid the noise of everyday life? Here's a simple way to tune in to his voice daily:

Take a few minutes to review your day with Jesus. Imagine the events of your day, reflecting on your attitudes, thoughts, interactions, and decisions. Ask Jesus, When was I listening to your voice? When did I struggle to hear your voice? Talk to him about what you've learned—and listen for his response.*

---

* This is adapted from the Daily Check-In in the Spiritual Exercises in Everyday Life, Seattle, Washington, cited in Elizabeth Liebert, *The Way of Discernment: Spiritual Practices for Decision Making* (Louisville: Westminster John Knox Press, 2008), 4–5.

Proverbs 20

¹ *Wine is a mocker and beer a brawler;*
  whoever is led astray by them is not wise.

² A king's wrath strikes terror like the roar of a lion;
  those who anger him forfeit their lives.

³ It is to one's honor to avoid strife,
  but every fool is quick to quarrel.

⁴ Sluggards do not plow in season;
  so at harvest time they look but find nothing.

⁵ The purposes of a person's heart are deep waters,
  but one who has insight draws them out.

⁶ Many claim to have unfailing love,
  but a faithful person who can find?

⁷ The righteous lead blameless lives;
  blessed are their children after them.

⁸ When a king sits on his throne to judge,
  he winnows out all evil with his eyes.

⁹ Who can say, "I have kept my heart pure;
   I am clean and without sin"?

¹⁰ Differing weights and differing measures—
   The Lᴏʀᴅ detests them both.

¹¹ Even small children are known by their
   actions,
   so is their conduct really pure and upright?

¹² Ears that hear and eyes that see—
   The Lᴏʀᴅ has made them both.

¹³ Do not love sleep or you will grow poor;
   stay awake and you will have food to spare.

¹⁴ "It's no good, it's no good!" says the buyer—
   then goes off and boasts about the pur-
   chase.

¹⁵ Gold there is, and rubies in abundance,
   but lips that speak knowledge are a rare
   jewel.

¹⁶ Take the garment of one who puts up
   security for a stranger;
   hold it in pledge if it is done for an outsider.

¹⁷ Food gained by fraud tastes sweet,
   but one ends up with a mouth full of gravel.

¹⁸ Plans are established by seeking advice;
   so if you wage war, obtain guidance.

¹⁹ A gossip betrays a confidence;
   so avoid anyone who talks too much.

²⁰ If someone curses their father or mother,
   their lamp will be snuffed out in pitch
   darkness.

²¹ An inheritance claimed too soon
   will not be blessed at the end.

²² Do not say, "I'll pay you back for this
   wrong!"
   Wait for the Lᴏʀᴅ, and he will avenge you.

²³ The Lᴏʀᴅ detests differing weights,
   and dishonest scales do not please him.

²⁴ A person's steps are directed by the Lᴏʀᴅ.
   How then can anyone understand their
   own way?

²⁵ It is a trap to dedicate something rashly
   and only later to consider one's vows.

²⁶ A wise king winnows out the wicked;
   he drives the threshing wheel over them.

²⁷ The human spirit is the lamp of the Lᴏʀᴅ
   that sheds light on one's inmost being.

²⁸ Love and faithfulness keep a king safe;
   through love his throne is made secure.

²⁹ The glory of young men is their strength,
   gray hair the splendor of the old.

³⁰ Blows and wounds scrub away evil,
   and beatings purge the inmost being. ❧

Someone to Trust

—MONICA LA ROSE

Many claim to have unfailing love,
but a faithful person who can find?

PROVERBS 20:6

"I just can't trust anyone," my friend said through tears. "Every time I do, they hurt me." Her story angered me—an ex-boyfriend, whom she really thought she could trust, had started spreading rumors about her as soon as they broke up. Struggling to trust again after a pain-filled childhood, this betrayal seemed just one more confirmation that people could not be trusted.

I struggled to find words that would comfort. One thing I could not say was that she was wrong about how hard it is to find someone to fully trust, that most people are completely kind and trustworthy. Her story was painfully familiar, reminding me of moments of unexpected betrayal in my own life. In fact, Scripture is very candid about human nature. In Proverbs 20:6, the author voices the same lament as my friend, forever memorializing the pain of betrayal.

What I could say is that the cruelty of others is only part of the story. Although wounds from others are real and painful, Jesus has made genuine love possible. In John 13:35, Jesus told his disciples that the world would know they were his followers because of their love. Although some people may still hurt us, because of Jesus there will also always be those who, freely sharing his love, will unconditionally support and care for us. Resting in his unfailing love, may we find healing, community, and courage to love others as he did. 🐚

LOVE [chesed] (v. 6)

Chesed can be translated *love, kindness, loyalty,* or *mercy*. About 75 percent of the 240 times the Old Testament uses *chesed*, it's related to God's *chesed* love for us. To understand the intensity of *chesed* love, imagine you are attending a wedding and it's time for the vows. You watch the couple promise to take each other "for better, for worse, for richer, for poorer, in sickness and health, until death do us part." They have just expressed *chesed* love. Their love is *loyal* (a vow to support each other whatever comes, "in sickness and health"). It's also *lasting* (at least "until death do us part"). Likewise, God's *chesed* love for us is a loyal, committed love (Psalm 136; Deuteronomy 7:9)—one that extends into all of eternity.

How have you been healed from past pain or trauma? Where do you still desire restoration and healing in your life?

How has God shown his faithfulness to you?

In what ways is God calling you to show his unconditional love to someone else?

Take time to talk with him about it.

—PRAY—

Jesus, I sometimes hurt. I confess this broken world often leaves me reeling, whether from disappointments, suffering and illnesses, unmet expectations, broken relationships, or regrets. I am also all too aware of my own failings, the ways in which I betray you, others, and myself through my thoughts and actions or omissions to act.

I desperately need you. Thank you for seeing me, for understanding me— for simply listening. In my darkest moments, you've shared in my pain and suffering, experiencing it with me. You have always been with me, my faithful friend.

Jesus, please heal the damaged places in my heart. Some of these wounds are deep, and I desperately need your loving, gentle, transforming care.

Finally, give me the courage to offer the loyal love you've freely given me to others.

In Jesus's name, Amen.

Proverbs 21

[1] *In the Lord's hand the king's heart is a stream of water*
that he channels toward all who please him.

[2] A person may think their own ways are right,
but the LORD weighs the heart.

[3] To do what is right and just
is more acceptable to the LORD than sacrifice.

[4] Haughty eyes and a proud heart—
the unplowed field of the wicked—produce sin.

[5] The plans of the diligent lead to profit
as surely as haste leads to poverty.

[6] A fortune made by a lying tongue
is a fleeting vapor and a deadly snare.

[7] The violence of the wicked will drag them away,
for they refuse to do what is right.

[8] The way of the guilty is devious,
but the conduct of the innocent is upright.

⁹ Better to live on a corner of the roof
than share a house with a quarrelsome wife.

¹⁰ The wicked crave evil;
their neighbors get no mercy from them.

¹¹ When a mocker is punished, the simple gain
wisdom;
by paying attention to the wise they get
knowledge.

¹² The Righteous One takes note of the house of
the wicked
and brings the wicked to ruin.

¹³ Whoever shuts their ears to the cry of the
poor
will also cry out and not be answered.

¹⁴ A gift given in secret soothes anger,
and a bribe concealed in the cloak pacifies
great wrath.

¹⁵ When justice is done, it brings joy to the
righteous
but terror to evildoers.

¹⁶ Whoever strays from the path of prudence
comes to rest in the company of the dead.

¹⁷ Whoever loves pleasure will become poor;
whoever loves wine and olive oil will never
be rich.

¹⁸ The wicked become a ransom for the
righteous,
and the unfaithful for the upright.

¹⁹ Better to live in a desert
than with a quarrelsome and nagging wife.

²⁰ The wise store up choice food and olive oil,
but fools gulp theirs down.

²¹ Whoever pursues righteousness and love
finds life, prosperity and honor.

²² One who is wise can go up against the city of
the mighty
and pull down the stronghold in which they
trust.

²³ Those who guard their mouths and their
tongues
keep themselves from calamity.

²⁴ The proud and arrogant person—"Mocker" is
his name—
behaves with insolent fury.

²⁵ The craving of a sluggard will be the death of
him,
because his hands refuse to work.

²⁶ All day long he craves for more,
but the righteous give without sparing.

²⁷ The sacrifice of the wicked is detestable—
how much more so when brought with evil
intent!

²⁸ A false witness will perish,
but a careful listener will testify successfully.

²⁹ The wicked put up a bold front,
but the upright give thought to their ways.

³⁰ There is no wisdom, no insight, no plan
that can succeed against the LORD.

³¹ The horse is made ready for the day of battle,
but victory rests with the LORD. ❧

Into Battle

—PATRICIA RAYBON

*The horse is made ready for the day of battle,
but victory rests with the LORD.*

PROVERBS 21:31

The wounded horse was named Drummer Boy. The animal, one of 112 mounts carrying British soldiers into battle during the famed Charge of the Light Brigade, showed such bravery and stamina that his assigned commander, Lieutenant Colonel de Salis, decided his horse deserved a medal as much as his valiant men. This was done even though their military action against enemy forces failed. Yet the cavalry's valor, matched by the courage of their horses, established the clash as one of Britain's greatest military moments, still celebrated today.

The confrontation, however, shows the wisdom of an ancient Bible proverb: "The horse is made ready for the day of battle, but victory rests with the LORD" (Proverbs 21:31). Scripture affirms this principle clearly. "For the LORD your God is the one who goes with you to fight for you against your enemies to give you victory" (Deuteronomy 20:4). Indeed, even against "the sting of death," wrote the apostle Paul. "Thanks be to God! He gives us the victory through our Lord Jesus Christ" (1 Corinthians 15:56–57).

Knowing this, our task still is to be prepared for life's tough tests. To build a ministry, we study, work, and pray. To create beautiful art, we master a skill. To conquer a mountain, we secure our tools and build our strength. Then, prepared, we're more than conquerors through Christ's strong love. 🐚

VICTORY BELONGS TO GOD

The horse is made ready for the day of battle, but victory rests with the LORD. —Proverbs 21:31

In the ancient world, the horse was a symbol of power. They provided the speed for the most feared weapon of ancient warfare—the chariot. With horse-drawn chariots, armies overran entire regions, instilling terror wherever they went. Proverbs 21:31 says that God gives victory, not superior military strength, however. Consider Judges 4–5 in which the prophet Deborah and the general Barak led an untrained militia of farmers on foot against 900 chariots—and prevailed!

When it comes to fulfilling God's purposes, he's less concerned with our having influence, power, and innovation on our side. He's looking for people whose hearts are fully committed to him (2 Chronicles 16:9).

GOD IN PROVERBS *insight*

The name of the Lord (*Yahweh*) is used eighty-seven times in Proverbs to give source, story, spirit, and context to the wisdom of these proverbs. The Lord of Israel's exodus, wilderness, exile, and messianic hope wants us to know that he's the beginning and end of all true wisdom and knowledge (2:6). The God of Solomon's insight can be trusted to turn even common sense into timely perspective and actions that help us while giving honor to him (3:5–7).

What battles has God fought on your behalf? Or when has he rescued you in a time of need?

What battles or challenges are you preparing for now?

If your victory rests in God, why should you prepare for a life test?

Proverbs 22

¹*A good name is more desirable than great riches;*
  to be esteemed is better than silver or gold.

²Rich and poor have this in common:
  The LORD is the Maker of them all.

³The prudent see danger and take refuge,
  but the simple keep going and pay the penalty.

⁴Humility is the fear of the LORD;
  its wages are riches and honor and life.

⁵In the paths of the wicked are snares and pitfalls,
  but those who would preserve their life stay far
  from them.

⁶Start children off on the way they should go,
  and even when they are old they will not turn
  from it.

⁷ The rich rule over the poor,
   and the borrower is slave to the lender.

⁸ Whoever sows injustice reaps calamity,
   and the rod they wield in fury will be
   broken.

⁹ The generous will themselves be blessed,
   for they share their food with the poor.

¹⁰ Drive out the mocker, and out goes strife;
   quarrels and insults are ended.

¹¹ One who loves a pure heart and who speaks
   with grace
   will have the king for a friend.

¹² The eyes of the LORD keep watch over
   knowledge,
   but he frustrates the words of the
   unfaithful.

¹³ The sluggard says, "There's a lion outside!
   I'll be killed in the public square!"

¹⁴ The mouth of an adulterous woman is a
   deep pit;
   a man who is under the LORD's wrath falls
   into it.

¹⁵ Folly is bound up in the heart of a child,
   but the rod of discipline will drive it far
   away.

¹⁶ One who oppresses the poor to increase his
   wealth
   and one who gives gifts to the rich—both
   come to poverty.

¹⁷ Pay attention and turn your ear to the
   sayings of the wise;
   apply your heart to what I teach,
¹⁸ for it is pleasing when you keep them in
   your heart
   and have all of them ready on your lips.
¹⁹ So that your trust may be in the LORD,
   I teach you today, even you.
²⁰ Have I not written thirty sayings for you,
   sayings of counsel and knowledge,
²¹ teaching you to be honest and to speak the
   truth,
   so that you bring back truthful reports
   to those you serve?

²² Do not exploit the poor because they are
   poor
   and do not crush the needy in court,
²³ for the LORD will take up their case
   and will exact life for life.

²⁴ Do not make friends with a hot-tempered
   person,
   do not associate with one easily angered,
²⁵ or you may learn their ways
   and get yourself ensnared.

²⁶ Do not be one who shakes hands in pledge
   or puts up security for debts;
²⁷ if you lack the means to pay,
   your very bed will be snatched from under
   you.

²⁸ Do not move an ancient boundary stone
   set up by your ancestors.

²⁹ Do you see someone skilled in their work?
   They will serve before kings;
   they will not serve before officials of low
   rank. ❧

Lessons for Little Ones

—JENNIFER BENSON SCHULDT

Start children off on the way they should go.

PROVERBS 22:6

What ways can you help a child deepen his or her faith in God?

When my daughter described a problem she was having in the school lunchroom, I immediately wondered how I could fix the issue for her. But then another thought occurred. Maybe God had allowed the problem so she could see him at work and get to know him better. Instead of running to the rescue, I decided to pray with her. The trouble cleared up without any help from me!

This situation showed my little one that God cares for her, that he listens when she prays, and that he answers prayers. The Bible says there's something significant about learning these lessons early in life. If we "start children off on the way they should go, . . . when they are old they will not turn from it" (Proverbs 22:6). When we start kids off with an awareness of Jesus and his power, we are giving them a place to return to if they wander and a foundation for spiritual growth throughout their lives.

Who has mentored you in faith, whether formally or informally? What is something you would like to emulate from his or her life or style of mentoring?

Consider how you might foster faith in a child. Point out God's design in nature, tell a story about how he has helped you, or invite a little one to thank God with you when things go right. God can work through you to tell of his goodness throughout all generations.

insight

FAMILY MATTERS

While most of the Old Testament tells the story of the nation of Israel, Proverbs has a sharper focus—that of the family. The opening, chapters 1 through 9, suggests it's a book of life lessons from a father figure to his son or young disciple, and, throughout, the book concerns itself with everyday people and their spheres at home with family, at work, and in relationship with their local community. In the book of Proverbs, we discover God pays attention to—and deeply cares about—the dealings of the family.

THIRTY SAYINGS OF THE WISE

Proverbs 22:17–24:22 is marked out as a separate section with the prologue, "Thirty Sayings of the Wise." Some scholars have argued that Solomon "borrowed" some of these proverbs from an ancient Egyptian wisdom work "The Instruction of Amenemope," which has thirty chapters. Regardless of its source, we believe that these Thirty Sayings are "God-breathed" (2 Timothy 3:16–17).

Proverbs 23

¹*When you sit to dine with a ruler,*

> note well what is before you,
> ² and put a knife to your throat
>   if you are given to gluttony.
> ³ Do not crave his delicacies,
>   for that food is deceptive.

> ⁴ Do not wear yourself out to get rich;
>   do not trust your own cleverness.
> ⁵ Cast but a glance at riches, and they are gone,
>   for they will surely sprout wings
>   and fly off to the sky like an eagle.

> ⁶ Do not eat the food of a begrudging host,
>   do not crave his delicacies;
> ⁷ for he is the kind of person
>   who is always thinking about the cost.
> "Eat and drink," he says to you,
>   but his heart is not with you.
> ⁸ You will vomit up the little you have eaten
>   and will have wasted your compliments.

⁹ Do not speak to fools,
　　for they will scorn your prudent words.

¹⁰ Do not move an ancient boundary stone
　　or encroach on the fields of the fatherless,
¹¹ for their Defender is strong;
　　he will take up their case against you.

¹² Apply your heart to instruction
　　and your ears to words of knowledge.

¹³ Do not withhold discipline from a child;
　　if you punish them with the rod, they will not die.
¹⁴ Punish them with the rod
　　and save them from death.

¹⁵ My son, if your heart is wise,
　　then my heart will be glad indeed;
¹⁶ my inmost being will rejoice
　　when your lips speak what is right.

¹⁷ Do not let your heart envy sinners,
　　but always be zealous for the fear of the LORD.
¹⁸ There is surely a future hope for you,
　　and your hope will not be cut off.

¹⁹ Listen, my son, and be wise,
　　and set your heart on the right path:
²⁰ Do not join those who drink too much wine
　　or gorge themselves on meat,
²¹ for drunkards and gluttons become poor,
　　and drowsiness clothes them in rags.

²² Listen to your father, who gave you life,
and do not despise your mother when she is old.
²³ Buy the truth and do not sell it—
wisdom, instruction and insight as well.
²⁴ The father of a righteous child has great joy;
a man who fathers a wise son rejoices in him.
²⁵ May your father and mother rejoice;
may she who gave you birth be joyful!

²⁶ My son, give me your heart
and let your eyes delight in my ways,
²⁷ for an adulterous woman is a deep pit,
and a wayward wife is a narrow well.
²⁸ Like a bandit she lies in wait
and multiplies the unfaithful among men.

²⁹ Who has woe? Who has sorrow?
Who has strife? Who has complaints?
Who has needless bruises? Who has bloodshot eyes?
³⁰ Those who linger over wine,
who go to sample bowls of mixed wine.
³¹ Do not gaze at wine when it is red,
when it sparkles in the cup,
when it goes down smoothly!
³² In the end it bites like a snake
and poisons like a viper.
³³ Your eyes will see strange sights,
and your mind will imagine confusing things.
³⁴ You will be like one sleeping on the high seas,
lying on top of the rigging.
³⁵ "They hit me," you will say, "but I'm not hurt!
They beat me, but I don't feel it!
When will I wake up
so I can find another drink?" ❧

Working off Bad Information

—WINN COLLIER

*Apply you heart to instruction
and your ears to words of knowledge.*

PROVERBS 23:12

On a recent trip to New York City, my wife and I wanted to brave a snowy evening and hire a taxi for a three-mile ride from our hotel to a Cuban restaurant. After entering the details into the taxi service's app, I gulped hard when the screen revealed the price for our short jaunt: $1,547.26. After recovering from the shock, I realized I had mistakenly requested a ride to our home—several hundred miles away!

If you're working with the wrong information, you're going to end up with disastrous results. Always. This is why Proverbs encourages us to "apply [our] heart to instruction and [our] ears to words of knowledge"—God's wisdom (Proverbs 23:12). If we instead seek advice from those who are foolish, those who pretend to know more than they do and who have turned their back on God, we'll be in trouble. They "scorn . . . prudent words" (v. 9) and can lead us astray with unhelpful, misguided, or even deceptive advice.

Instead, we can bend our "ears to words of knowledge" (v. 12). We can open our heart and receive God's liberating instruction, words of clarity and hope. When we listen to those who know the deep ways of God, they help us receive and follow divine wisdom. And God's wisdom will never lead us astray but always encourages and leads us toward life and wholeness. 🌱

INSTRUCTION

[*musar*] (v. 12)

Embedded in the idea of *instruction* (*musar*) is good news—it's OK to fail! In fact, missteps are at the heart of the process of becoming wise (10:17; 15:31). In Proverbs, *musar* most often refers to discipline—the consequences from our choices or God's correction when we fall short (23:13; 24:32; 3:11–12). However, Proverbs says that God only disciplines "those he loves," as a parent disciplines their beloved children—to help them grow (3:12). Through providing *discipline*, God helps us mature into the people we were created to be . . . if we can open-heartedly confront our mistakes and humbly learn from them (15:33; 18:12; 22:4).

When was a time that you were working off bad information? How did that end up?

What advice do you need from God today? Take time to ask him for direction.

insight

WORKING OFF GOOD INFORMATION

At life's crossroads, how do you make decisions? Sometimes it's helpful to recognize and write down your spiritual landmarks—the places in your journey God has guided and directed you powerfully.* By creating a kind of spiritual map or story, you can remember how God communicates, moves, and speaks to you personally, helping you to discern his voice in your current situation. But he often works in new ways—so be ready for surprises too!

---

* Margaret Silf, *Inner Compass: An Invitation to Ignatian Spirituality* (Chicago: Loyola Press, 1999), 35–50.

Proverbs 24

¹*Do not envy the wicked,*

>   do not desire their company;
> ²for their hearts plot violence,
>   and their lips talk about making trouble.

³By wisdom a house is built,
>   and through understanding it is established;
⁴through knowledge its rooms are filled
>   with rare and beautiful treasures.

⁵The wise prevail through great power,
>   and those who have knowledge muster their strength.
⁶Surely you need guidance to wage war,
>   and victory is won through many advisers.

⁷Wisdom is too high for fools;
>   in the assembly at the gate they must not open their
>   mouths.

⁸ Whoever plots evil
   will be known as a schemer.
⁹ The schemes of folly are sin,
   and people detest a mocker.

¹⁰ If you falter in a time of trouble,
   how small is your strength!
¹¹ Rescue those being led away to death;
   hold back those staggering toward slaughter.
¹² If you say, "But we knew nothing about this,"
   does not he who weighs the heart perceive it?
Does not he who guards your life know it?
   Will he not repay everyone according to what they have done?

¹³ Eat honey, my son, for it is good;
   honey from the comb is sweet to your taste.
¹⁴ Know also that wisdom is like honey for you:
   If you find it, there is a future hope for you,
   and your hope will not be cut off.

¹⁵ Do not lurk like a thief near the house of the righteous,
   do not plunder their dwelling place;
¹⁶ for though the righteous fall seven times, they rise again,
   but the wicked stumble when calamity strikes.

¹⁷ Do not gloat when your enemy falls;
   when they stumble, do not let your heart rejoice,
¹⁸ or the LORD will see and disapprove
   and turn his wrath away from them.

¹⁹ Do not fret because of evildoers
   or be envious of the wicked,
²⁰ for the evildoer has no future hope,
   and the lamp of the wicked will be snuffed out.

²¹ Fear the LORD and the king, my son,
   and do not join with rebellious officials,
²² for those two will send sudden destruction on them,
   and who knows what calamities they can bring?

²³ These also are sayings of the wise:

> To show partiality in judging is not good:
> ²⁴ Whoever says to the guilty, "You are innocent,"
>   will be cursed by peoples and denounced by nations.
> ²⁵ But it will go well with those who convict the guilty,
>   and rich blessing will come on them.

> ²⁶ An honest answer
>   is like a kiss on the lips.

> ²⁷ Put your outdoor work in order
>   and get your fields ready;
>   after that, build your house.

²⁸ Do not testify against your neighbor without cause—
    would you use your lips to mislead?
²⁹ Do not say, "I'll do to them as they have done to me;
    I'll pay them back for what they did."

³⁰ I went past the field of a sluggard,
    past the vineyard of someone who has no sense;
³¹ thorns had come up everywhere,
    the ground was covered with weeds,
    and the stone wall was in ruins.
³² I applied my heart to what I observed
    and learned a lesson from what I saw:
³³ A little sleep, a little slumber,
    a little folding of the hands to rest—
³⁴ and poverty will come on you like a thief
    and scarcity like an armed man.

Good for You

—KIRSTEN HOLMBERG

Wisdom is like honey for you:
If you find it, there is a future hope.

PROVERBS 24:14

People the world over spent an estimated $98.2 billion on chocolate in 2016. The number is staggering, yet at the same time not all that surprising. Chocolate, after all, tastes delicious and we enjoy consuming it. So the world rejoiced collectively when the sweet treat was found to have significant health benefits as well. Chocolate contains flavonoids that help safeguard the body against aging and heart disease. Never has a prescription for health been so well received or heeded (in moderation, of course)!

Solomon suggested there's another "sweet" worthy of our investment: wisdom. He recommended his son eat honey "for it is good" (Proverbs 24:13) and compared its sweetness to wisdom. The person who feeds on God's wisdom in Scripture finds it not only sweet to the soul but beneficial for teaching and training, equipping us for "every good work" we'll need to accomplish in life (2 Timothy 3:16–17).

Wisdom is what allows us to make smart choices and understand the world around us. And it's worth investing in and sharing with those we love—as Solomon wished to do for his son. We can feel good about feasting on God's wisdom in the Bible. It's a sweet treat that we can enjoy without limit—in fact, we're encouraged to! God, thank you for the sweetness of your Scriptures! 🐝

THE GIFT OF WISDOM

In the New Testament, the ability to make wise choices—discernment—is a spiritual gift (1 Corinthians 12:4–10). Like other spiritual gifts, discernment is both God-given and intended to strengthen the community of faith. If you have the gift of discernment, you are called to help the church listen to God's voice and know his heart. While some are particularly gifted in discernment, the apostle Paul says that we all have access to God's wisdom (Romans 12:2).

HOPE [*tiqva*] (v. 14)

In the Old Testament, hope—*tiqva* in Hebrew—literally means "cord" (see Rahab's use of a scarlet *tiqva* in Joshua 2). The biblical idea of hope relates to the cord too—and can revolutionize our understanding of the concept. The cord can bear substantial weight when fastened to a strong surface; if the foundation to which the cord is tied is unstable, however, the cord will give way.

As humans, we tie our hope to a variety of things: maybe our abilities, achievements, relationships, or even our own virtue. While all good things, they are flimsy anchors. We live in a fallen world, and finding ultimate hope in anything in it is bound to come apart. Throughout the Old Testament, God calls his people to tie their *tiqva* to him. Likewise, when we secure our hope to the One who is all-powerful, all-knowing, and completely trustworthy—we find safety and rest.

—PRAY—

Jesus, thank you for your wisdom. It is sweet to the taste, giving me direction, protection, and power. Your guidance makes my way straight.

I often seek to manage situations, people, things, and responsibilities on my own—sometimes tying my hope to them. But I know that finding ultimate hope in anything apart from you is bound to unravel. Help me fasten my hope to you, for it is in you alone that I find safety and peace.

In Jesus's name, Amen.

What wisdom do you need to consume today?

How has God's wisdom been sweet to you?

As you read chapter 24, what proverb attracts your attention?
Take time to listen to God's invitation for you through the proverb.

Proverbs 25

¹ *These are more proverbs of Solomon,*
   compiled by the men of Hezekiah king of Judah:

² It is the glory of God to conceal a matter;
   to search out a matter is the glory of kings.
³ As the heavens are high and the earth is deep,
   so the hearts of kings are unsearchable.

⁴ Remove the dross from the silver,
   and a silversmith can produce a vessel;
⁵ remove wicked officials from the king's presence,
   and his throne will be established through righteousness.

⁶ Do not exalt yourself in the king's presence,
   and do not claim a place among his great men;
⁷ it is better for him to say to you, "Come up here,"
   than for him to humiliate you before his nobles.

What you have seen with your eyes
   ⁸ do not bring hastily to court,
for what will you do in the end
   if your neighbor puts you to shame?

⁹ If you take your neighbor to court,
  do not betray another's confidence,
¹⁰ or the one who hears it may shame you
  and the charge against you will stand.

¹¹ Like apples of gold in settings of silver
  is a ruling rightly given.
¹² Like an earring of gold or an ornament of
    fine gold
  is the rebuke of a wise judge to a listening
    ear.

¹³ Like a snow-cooled drink at harvest time
  is a trustworthy messenger to the one who
    sends him;
  he refreshes the spirit of his master.
¹⁴ Like clouds and wind without rain
  is one who boasts of gifts never given.

¹⁵ Through patience a ruler can be persuaded,
  and a gentle tongue can break a bone.

¹⁶ If you find honey, eat just enough—
  too much of it, and you will vomit.
¹⁷ Seldom set foot in your neighbor's house—
  too much of you, and they will hate you.

¹⁸ Like a club or a sword or a sharp arrow
  is one who gives false testimony against a
    neighbor.
¹⁹ Like a broken tooth or a lame foot
  is reliance on the unfaithful in a time of
    trouble.

²⁰ Like one who takes away a garment on a
    cold day,
  or like vinegar poured on a wound,
  is one who sings songs to a heavy heart.

²¹ If your enemy is hungry, give him food to
    eat;
  if he is thirsty, give him water to drink.
²² In doing this, you will heap burning coals
    on his head,
  and the LORD will reward you.

²³ Like a north wind that brings unexpected
    rain
  is a sly tongue—which provokes a
    horrified look.

²⁴ Better to live on a corner of the roof
  than share a house with a quarrelsome
    wife.

²⁵ Like cold water to a weary soul
  is good news from a distant land.
²⁶ Like a muddied spring or a polluted well
  are the righteous who give way to the
    wicked.

²⁷ It is not good to eat too much honey,
  nor is it honorable to search out matters
    that are too deep.

²⁸ Like a city whose walls are broken through
  is a person who lacks self-control. 🐀

Timely Words

—MARVIN WILLIAMS

Like apples of gold in settings of silver is a ruling rightly given.

PROVERBS 25:11

You may have heard the adage, "Timing is everything." According to the Bible, good timing applies to our words and speech too. Think of a time when God used you to bring a timely word to refresh someone, or when you wanted to speak, but it was wiser for you to remain silent.

The Bible says that there is an appropriate time to speak (Ecclesiastes 3:7). Solomon compared properly timed and well-spoken words with golden apples in a silver setting—beautiful, valuable, and carefully crafted (Proverbs 25:11–12). Knowing the right time to speak is beneficial for both the speaker and hearer, whether they are words of love, encouragement, or rebuke. Keeping silent also has its place and time. When tempted to deride, belittle, or slander a neighbor, Solomon said that it is wise to hold our tongue, recognizing the appropriate time for silence (11:12–13). When talkativeness or anger tempts us to sin against God or another human being, resistance comes by being slow to speak (10:19; James 1:19).

It's often hard to know what to say and when to say it. The Spirit will help us to be discerning. He will help us use the right words at the right time and in the right manner, for the good of others and for his honor. 🐚

When have you experienced God's prompting to speak a timely word? When has God called you to listen to someone without offering advice?

How is the Spirit nudging you currently to either speak or be silent?

Whom do you admire for his or her wisdom?

WORD PICTURES IN PROVERBS

The analogies in Proverbs offer colorful—sometimes shocking—word pictures (vv. 11–14). More than *telling* us about a truth, they *show* it to us—so that we cannot avoid it. For example, consider one of Proverb's most famous analogies: "A beautiful woman who lacks discretion is like a gold ring in a pig's snout" (11:22 NLT). What an effective (if jarring) way to communicate the need for wisdom. Analogies like this one wake us up to the truth—fast.

See if you can identify some of the analogies in today's chapter (if you spot the word *like*, you have found an analogy).

insight

WHEN WAS PROVERBS WRITTEN?

The short answer: *We don't know!* King Solomon commissioned the book during his reign (tenth century BC). However, it wasn't completed *at least* until several hundred years later—when Hezekiah was king of Judah (around 700 BC), and many scholars believe the manuscript was finalized many years after Hezekiah's time.

In today's Bible reading, the author writes that King Hezekiah's court assembled a compilation of Solomon's proverbs (v. 1). It's not surprising that Hezekiah, who led his people in worship of Yahweh (2 Kings 18:5–7), would have desired to further Solomon's work about fearing God (9:10).

— PRAY —

Jesus, I ask for your guidance as I interact with others today. Help me to recognize their needs and concerns. Even when I'm with others, I ask to be attuned to you and to your guidance—to know when to speak and when to listen.

Your grace is sufficient for me when I am afraid to share or don't have the perfect words to say. Especially in my weakness, you have room to work through me. So I thank you for going before me in my every interaction, empowering me to carry out the good work which you have planned for me in advance (Ephesians 2:10).

May you be glorified in and through me.

In Jesus's name, Amen.

Proverbs 26

¹ *Like snow in summer or rain in harvest,*
  honor is not fitting for a fool.
² Like a fluttering sparrow or a darting swallow,
  an undeserved curse does not come to rest.
³ A whip for the horse, a bridle for the donkey,
  and a rod for the backs of fools!
⁴ Do not answer a fool according to his folly,
  or you yourself will be just like him.
⁵ Answer a fool according to his folly,
  or he will be wise in his own eyes.
⁶ Sending a message by the hands of a fool
  is like cutting off one's feet or drinking poison.
⁷ Like the useless legs of one who is lame
  is a proverb in the mouth of a fool.
⁸ Like tying a stone in a sling
  is the giving of honor to a fool.
⁹ Like a thornbush in a drunkard's hand
  is a proverb in the mouth of a fool.

¹⁰ Like an archer who wounds at random
   is one who hires a fool or any passer-by.
¹¹ As a dog returns to its vomit,
   so fools repeat their folly.
¹² Do you see a person wise in their own eyes?
   There is more hope for a fool than for them.

¹³ A sluggard says, "There's a lion in the road,
   a fierce lion roaming the streets!"
¹⁴ As a door turns on its hinges,
   so a sluggard turns on his bed.
¹⁵ A sluggard buries his hand in the dish;
   he is too lazy to bring it back to his mouth.
¹⁶ A sluggard is wiser in his own eyes
   than seven people who answer discreetly.

¹⁷ Like one who grabs a stray dog by the ears
   is someone who rushes into a quarrel not
      their own.

¹⁸ Like a maniac shooting
   flaming arrows of death
¹⁹ is one who deceives their neighbor
   and says, "I was only joking!"

²⁰ Without wood a fire goes out;
   without a gossip a quarrel dies down.
²¹ As charcoal to embers and as wood to fire,
   so is a quarrelsome person for kindling
      strife.
²² The words of a gossip are like choice
      morsels;
   they go down to the inmost parts.

²³ Like a coating of silver dross on earthenware
   are fervent lips with an evil heart.

²⁴ Enemies disguise themselves with their lips,
   but in their hearts they harbor deceit.
²⁵ Though their speech is charming, do not
      believe them,
   for seven abominations fill their hearts.
²⁶ Their malice may be concealed by
      deception,
   but their wickedness will be exposed in the
      assembly.
²⁷ Whoever digs a pit will fall into it;
   if someone rolls a stone, it will roll back on
      them.
²⁸ A lying tongue hates those it hurts,
   and a flattering mouth works ruin. ❧

When the Fire Goes Out

—DAVID H. ROPER

Without wood a fire goes out;
without a gossip a quarrel dies down.

PROVERBS 26:20

When a fire finishes burning through the material it feeds on, it goes out. Similarly, when gossip reaches the ear of someone who will not repeat it, it dies.

Gossip, like other sins, is like "tasty trifles" (Proverbs 26:22 NKJV). We like to hear it and share it with others because it "tastes" good. Gossip is rooted in our need to feel good about ourselves. As we bring others down, we gain the illusion that we are moving upward.

That's why spreading gossip is so difficult to resist. It takes prayer and God's grace to bring us to the point where we refuse to pass it on or even hear it—even under the guise of personal concern or a request to pray for a sinning friend in trouble.

We must ask God for the wisdom to know when to speak, what to speak, and when to simply keep our mouths shut. For "sin is not ended by multiplying words, but the prudent hold their tongues" (10:19).

It is often wise to be quiet and speak few words. But if we must speak, let's talk of those things that encourage and move others closer to God, not those things that will discourage and hurt them. "The tongue of the wise brings healing" (12:18).

How have you witnessed the power of words to be destructive or to bring about life*?*

In what situations do you find it challenging to resist the temptation to gossip*?*

How can you influence others to speak words of life*?*

insight

MEET THE FOOL
(vv. 1–12)

In the opening of Proverbs, the authors give everyone free access to wisdom—except the fool (1:4–5, 7).* The foolish person in Proverbs has precluded himself or herself from the invite; by definition, the fool doesn't want to learn (17:6; 15:5). Obstinate. Self-centered. Arrogant. Bombastic. These words describe the fool. Given these traits, the fool rarely welcomes constructive feedback. As we encounter the foolish person throughout Proverbs, we discover this person's biggest issue isn't his or her IQ. The fool scorns God—and listening to God is the way to become wise (1:29).

---

* Tremper Longman III, *How to Read Proverbs* (Downers Grover, IL: InterVarsity Press, 2002), chap. 1, Kindle.

—PRAY—

Jesus, I know the tongue is such a powerful instrument—something that can be used as a healing balm or a weapon. How sobering! Sometimes I'm amazed you could trust me with such an awesome responsibility as managing how I speak. Help me to wield this instrument well: To speak words of life, not death. To heal instead of harm. To encourage, not discourage. And to be courageous instead of timid.

I'm not perfect. Sometimes I'm not even aware of my tendency to be drawn into toxic conversations. Forgive me when I miss the mark.

I ask for your wisdom to know when to speak, what to speak, and when to simply keep my mouth shut.

In Jesus's name, Amen.

Proverbs 27

¹ Do not boast about tomorrow,
    for you do not know what a day may bring.

² Let someone else praise you, and not your own mouth;
    an outsider, and not your own lips.

³ Stone is heavy and sand a burden,
    but a fool's provocation is heavier than both.

⁴ Anger is cruel and fury overwhelming,
    but who can stand before jealousy?

⁵ Better is open rebuke
    than hidden love.

⁶ Wounds from a friend can be trusted,
    but an enemy multiplies kisses.

⁷ One who is full loathes honey from the comb,
    but to the hungry even what is bitter tastes sweet.

⁸ Like a bird that flees its nest
    is anyone who flees from home.

⁹ Perfume and incense bring joy to the heart,
and the pleasantness of a friend
springs from their heartfelt advice.

¹⁰ Do not forsake your friend or a friend of
your family,
and do not go to your relative's house when
disaster strikes you—
better a neighbor nearby than a relative far
away.

¹¹ Be wise, my son, and bring joy to my heart;
then I can answer anyone who treats me
with contempt.

¹² The prudent see danger and take refuge,
but the simple keep going and pay the
penalty.

¹³ Take the garment of one who puts up
security for a stranger;
hold it in pledge if it is done for an outsider.

¹⁴ If anyone loudly blesses their neighbor early
in the morning,
it will be taken as a curse.

¹⁵ A quarrelsome wife is like the dripping
of a leaky roof in a rainstorm;
¹⁶ restraining her is like restraining the wind
or grasping oil with the hand.

¹⁷ As iron sharpens iron,
so one person sharpens another.

¹⁸ The one who guards a fig tree will eat its
fruit,
and whoever protects their master will be
honored.

¹⁹ As water reflects the face,
so one's life reflects the heart.

²⁰ Death and Destruction are never satisfied,
and neither are human eyes.

²¹ The crucible for silver and the furnace for
gold,
but people are tested by their praise.

²² Though you grind a fool in a mortar,
grinding them like grain with a pestle,
you will not remove their folly from them.

²³ Be sure you know the condition of your
flocks,
give careful attention to your herds;
²⁴ for riches do not endure forever,
and a crown is not secure for all
generations.
²⁵ When the hay is removed and new growth
appears
and the grass from the hills is gathered in,
²⁶ the lambs will provide you with clothing,
and the goats with the price of a field.
²⁷ You will have plenty of goats' milk to feed
your family
and to nourish your female servants. ᔡ

God's Sandpaper

—AMY BOUCHER PYE

As iron sharpens iron, so one person sharpens another.

PROVERBS 27:17

My friend's words stung. Trying to sleep, I battled to stop mulling over her pointed comments about my strong opinions. As I lay there, I asked for God's wisdom and peace. Several weeks later, still concerned about the matter, I prayed, "I hurt, Lord, but show me where I need to change. Show me where she's right."

My friend had acted as God's sandpaper in my life. My feelings felt rubbed raw, but I sensed that how I responded would lead to the building of my character—or not. My choice was to submit to the smoothing process, confessing my pride and stubborn stance. I sensed that my bumps and imperfections didn't glorify the Lord.

King Solomon knew that life in community could be difficult, a theme he addressed in the book of Proverbs. In chapter 27, we see his wisdom applied to relationships. He likens the sharp words between friends as iron sharpening iron: "As iron sharpens iron, so one person sharpens another" (v. 17), shaving off the rough edges in each other's behavior. The process may bring about wounds, such as the hurt I felt from my friend's words (see v. 6), but ultimately the Lord can use these words to help and encourage us to make needed changes in our attitude and behavior.

How might the Lord be smoothing out your rough edges for his glory? 🌿

A TRUE FRIEND
IS AN HONEST ONE

Proverbs offers advice for finding a "friend that sticks closer than a brother" (18:24)—choose someone honest (24:26). Sincere friends can be our toughest critics. It's our acquaintances—even our enemies—who more often offer indiscriminate praise. The author of Proverbs explores this upside-down dynamic in today's chapter: "Wounds from a friend can be trusted, but an enemy multiplies kisses" (27:6).

Only honest friends are willing to risk their reputations—and the friendship—for our growth (v. 17). They care more about us than the security of the relationship.

PRAY

Jesus, this shaping process hurts,
but I want to submit to it.
Mold me and smooth me.
Give me a willing spirit to
receive the truth from those I love,
even if the message can sting
or cause me discomfort.
Thank you for friends who
are willing to be honest with me,
who want the best for me,
even if the truth hurts.

In Jesus's name, Amen.

How has God used a relationship in your life to sharpen your character? In what ways have you grown through this process?

How is God leading you to speak truth to— or to stand with— someone in your life?

As you read chapter 27, what proverb attracts your attention? Take time to listen to God's invitation for you through the proverb.

Proverbs 28

¹ *The wicked flee though no one pursues,*
>
> but the righteous are as bold as a lion.

² When a country is rebellious, it has many rulers,
> but a ruler with discernment and knowledge
> maintains order.

³ A ruler who oppresses the poor
> is like a driving rain that leaves no crops.

⁴ Those who forsake instruction praise the wicked,
> but those who heed it resist them.

⁵ Evildoers do not understand what is right,
> but those who seek the LORD understand it fully.

⁶ Better the poor whose walk is blameless
> than the rich whose ways are perverse.

⁷ A discerning son heeds instruction,
> but a companion of gluttons disgraces his father.

⁸ Whoever increases wealth by taking interest or
    profit from the poor
  amasses it for another, who will be kind to
    the poor.

⁹ If anyone turns a deaf ear to my instruction,
  even their prayers are detestable.

¹⁰ Whoever leads the upright along an evil path
  will fall into their own trap,
  but the blameless will receive a good inher-
    itance.

¹¹ The rich are wise in their own eyes;
  one who is poor and discerning sees how
    deluded they are.

¹² When the righteous triumph, there is great
    elation;
  but when the wicked rise to power, people go
    into hiding.

¹³ Whoever conceals their sins does not prosper,
  but the one who confesses and renounces
    them finds mercy.

¹⁴ Blessed is the one who always trembles before
    God,
  but whoever hardens their heart falls into
    trouble.

¹⁵ Like a roaring lion or a charging bear
  is a wicked ruler over a helpless people.

¹⁶ A tyrannical ruler practices extortion,
  but one who hates ill-gotten gain will enjoy a
    long reign.

¹⁷ Anyone tormented by the guilt of murder
  will seek refuge in the grave;
  let no one hold them back.

¹⁸ The one whose walk is blameless is kept safe,
  but the one whose ways are perverse will fall
    into the pit.

¹⁹ Those who work their land will have
    abundant food,
  but those who chase fantasies will have their
    fill of poverty.

²⁰ A faithful person will be richly blessed,
  but one eager to get rich will not go
    unpunished.

²¹ To show partiality is not good—
  yet a person will do wrong for a piece of
    bread.

²² The stingy are eager to get rich
  and are unaware that poverty awaits them.

²³ Whoever rebukes a person will in the end gain
    favor
  rather than one who has a flattering tongue.

²⁴ Whoever robs their father or mother
  and says, "It's not wrong,"
  is partner to one who destroys.

²⁵ The greedy stir up conflict,
  but those who trust in the Lord will prosper.

²⁶ Those who trust in themselves are fools,
  but those who walk in wisdom are kept safe.

²⁷ Those who give to the poor will lack nothing,
  but those who close their eyes to them
    receive many curses.

²⁸ When the wicked rise to power, people go
    into hiding;
  but when the wicked perish, the righteous
    thrive. ❧

How to Get Rid of Fear

—MART DEHAAN

The wicked flee
though no one pursues,
but the righteous
are as bold as a lion.

PROVERBS 28:1

The flashing sign along a stretch of North Carolina interstate warned: Slow Down! Drug Checkpoint Ahead.

About two hundred vehicles took the next exit—and were the only ones searched. The only drivers with reason to exit were residents or those avoiding the checkpoint! Authorities made several arrests and seized two cars that were transporting drugs.

A loss of courage is just one of the side effects of lawbreaking. The boldness required to break the law is soon replaced by the fear of getting caught. We find ourselves running even when no one is chasing us (Proverbs 28:1).

In Leviticus 26, God explicitly told his people what would happen if they chose to break his law. He warned that they would flee at "the sound of a windblown leaf" and they would run "even though no one is pursuing them" (Leviticus 26:36). But God left the door open for genuine repentance (vv. 40–42).

Do you have unconfessed sin causing you to hide from others or from God? If we admit our sins to God, he promises forgiveness. Confession is the first step to restoration (1 John 1:9). Your heavenly Father doesn't want you to be in hiding—but longs for you to find freedom and rest in him (Matthew 11:28–30).

Is there anything weighing down on you, whether anxiety, stress, or unconfessed sin?

How has God helped you take a risk or walk bravely? Where do you need his help in living boldly and powerfully today?

What are ways you can practice courage?

JESUS, THE WISDOM OF GOD

If you seek a model for wisdom, you only have to look at
Jesus. As the "image of the invisible God," Jesus is the repre-
sentation of God's wisdom on earth (Colossians 1:5). As a
young boy, Jesus internalized wisdom (Luke 2:52). During his
three-year ministry, Jesus confounded the religious leaders
and the people with his insights (Matthew 22:22; 13:54).
Following Jesus's death and resurrection, the apostle Paul
called Jesus the "wisdom from God" (1 Corinthians 1:30; also
see Colossians 2:3). Jesus is God's wisdom in human form.

MEET "THE *insight* RIGHTEOUS" (v. 1)

In everyday usage, the idea of a "righteous" person has taken
on certain connotations. We might envision, for example, a
righteous person as someone with an unusually strict and
rigid moral code for their personal behavior.

However, the Hebrew *tsadik*, which is translated "the
righteous," has a more holistic and practical meaning than
an individualistic moral code. "The righteous" in the Bible
are those committed to living in accordance with the divine
wisdom and justice embedded into reality by God. And the
righteous are those willing to pursue the shalom and wholeness God has intended for the world, even when it comes
at great personal cost, for "better to be poor and walk in
integrity than to be crooked in one's ways even though rich"
(28:6 NRSV).

As we soak in the wisdom found in Proverbs, we are chal-
lenged to expand our view of living with wisdom to include
a willingness to take a stand for—even stake our lives on—
the cause of true justice, for to do so reflects our loyalty to
God and our love for his world.

Proverbs 29

¹ *Whoever remains stiff-necked after many rebukes*
   will suddenly be destroyed—without remedy.

² When the righteous thrive, the people rejoice;
   when the wicked rule, the people groan.

³ A man who loves wisdom brings joy to his father,
   but a companion of prostitutes squanders his
      wealth.

⁴ By justice a king gives a country stability,
   but those who are greedy for bribes tear it down.

⁵ Those who flatter their neighbors
   are spreading nets for their feet.

⁶ Evildoers are snared by their own sin,
   but the righteous shout for joy and are glad.

⁷ The righteous care about justice for the poor,
   but the wicked have no such concern.

⁸ Mockers stir up a city,
    but the wise turn away anger.

⁹ If a wise person goes to court with a fool,
    the fool rages and scoffs, and there is no
        peace.

¹⁰ The bloodthirsty hate a person of integrity
    and seek to kill the upright.

¹¹ Fools give full vent to their rage,
    but the wise bring calm in the end.

¹² If a ruler listens to lies,
    all his officials become wicked.

¹³ The poor and the oppressor have this in
        common:
    The LORD gives sight to the eyes of both.

¹⁴ If a king judges the poor with fairness,
    his throne will be established forever.

¹⁵ A rod and a reprimand impart wisdom,
    but a child left undisciplined disgraces its
        mother.

¹⁶ When the wicked thrive, so does sin,
    but the righteous will see their downfall.

¹⁷ Discipline your children, and they will give
        you peace;
    they will bring you the delights you desire.

¹⁸ Where there is no revelation, people cast off
        restraint;
    but blessed is the one who heeds wisdom's
        instruction.

¹⁹ Servants cannot be corrected by mere
        words;
    though they understand, they will not
        respond.

²⁰ Do you see someone who speaks in haste?
    There is more hope for a fool than for them.

²¹ A servant pampered from youth
    will turn out to be insolent.

²² An angry person stirs up conflict,
    and a hot-tempered person commits many
        sins.

²³ Pride brings a person low,
    but the lowly in spirit gain honor.

²⁴ The accomplices of thieves are their own
        enemies;
    they are put under oath and dare not
        testify.

²⁵ Fear of man will prove to be a snare,
    but whoever trusts in the LORD is kept safe.

²⁶ Many seek an audience with a ruler,
    but it is from the LORD that one gets
        justice.

²⁷ The righteous detest the dishonest;
    the wicked detest the upright. ❧

Volcanic Activity

—CINDY HESS KASPER

An angry person stirs up conflict,
and a hot-tempered person commits many sins.

PROVERBS 29:22

It erupts. It melts everything in its path. Its blast is as powerful as a nuclear explosion!

Well, maybe not—but a temper can feel as intense as a volcano when it is aimed directly at another person in a family. The moment may be quickly over, but it can leave emotional devastation and bitter feelings behind.

It's sad that the people we love the most are often the target of our hurtful words. But even when we feel we've been provoked, we have a choice. Will we respond in anger or in kindness?

The Bible tells us to rid ourselves of bitterness, and to "be kind to one another, tenderhearted, forgiving one another, even as God in Christ forgave you" (Ephesians 4:32).

If you are struggling with chronic anger that is hurting your relationships, surrender this vulnerable part of your emotions to Christ's strength (Philippians 4:13). The path to forgiveness can be a long, hard-fought journey. As you grow, seek out help from others to learn how to deal with your strong, God-given emotions in appropriate ways. As we earnestly seek to love others and to please God, we can win the victory over a volcanic temper. 🍃

ANGER ['ap̄h] (v. 22)

Have you ever seen someone enraged, gasping for breath, their nostrils flaring? The ancient Israelites incorporated these bodily signs of fury into their word for *anger*: *'ap̄h* literally means "nose" or "nostrils" or "face." In the Old Testament, *anger* is coupled with the word *burn*, and a common expression in ancient Israel was literally "the nose burns"—meaning that someone was very angry (Genesis 30:2; Exodus 4:14). Anger is a vital, God-given emotion (Mark 3:1–6). In Proverbs, though, the "angry person" is a negative character—as this person's anger distorts his or her entire outlook and actions (15:18; 14:17).

insight

When have you seen or experienced anger as healing, redemptive, or transformative? When has it been unhealthy or destructive?

Is there anyone in your life who has wronged or hurt you whom you would like to forgive?

PRAY

Jesus, you created my capacity to experience anger and expressed your own anger openly (Matthew 21:12–13; Mark 11:15–18). Thank you for the way anger can be used to cleanse, purify, and make way for transformation—giving me the courage to stand against injustice and to seek renewal and change.

Like any other force, I know it has the power to create devastation. As I give voice to my anger, help me express it wisely. Let it be a tool in identifying evil, trauma, and the broken things in me and others, and, ultimately, a pathway to bring about healing in my relationships and in my life. May I not let it embitter me or destroy those closest to me.

May you be glorified in and through my expression of anger.

In Jesus's name, Amen.

Proverbs 30

¹ *The sayings of Agur son of Jakeh—*
an inspired utterance.

This man's utterance to Ithiel:

"I am weary, God,
  but I can prevail.
² Surely I am only a brute, not a man;
  I do not have human understanding.
³ I have not learned wisdom,
  nor have I attained to the knowledge of the Holy
    One.
⁴ Who has gone up to heaven and come down?
  Whose hands have gathered up the wind?
Who has wrapped up the waters in a cloak?
  Who has established all the ends of the earth?
What is his name, and what is the name of his son?
  Surely you know!

⁵ "Every word of God is flawless;
   he is a shield to those who take refuge in him.
⁶ Do not add to his words,
   or he will rebuke you and prove you a liar.

⁷ "Two things I ask of you, LORD;
   do not refuse me before I die:
⁸ Keep falsehood and lies far from me;
   give me neither poverty nor riches,
   but give me only my daily bread.
⁹ Otherwise, I may have too much and disown you
   and say, 'Who is the LORD?'
Or I may become poor and steal,
   and so dishonor the name of my God.

¹⁰ "Do not slander a servant to their master,
   or they will curse you, and you will pay for it.

¹¹ "There are those who curse their fathers
   and do not bless their mothers;
¹² those who are pure in their own eyes
   and yet are not cleansed of their filth;
¹³ those whose eyes are ever so haughty,
   whose glances are so disdainful;
¹⁴ those whose teeth are swords
   and whose jaws are set with knives
to devour the poor from the earth
   and the needy from among mankind.

¹⁵ "The leech has two daughters.
    'Give! Give!' they cry.

"There are three things that are never satisfied,
    four that never say, 'Enough!':
¹⁶ the grave, the barren womb,
    land, which is never satisfied with water,
    and fire, which never says, 'Enough!'

¹⁷ "The eye that mocks a father,
    that scorns an aged mother,
will be pecked out by the ravens of the valley,
    will be eaten by the vultures.

¹⁸ "There are three things that are too amazing for me,
    four that I do not understand:
¹⁹ the way of an eagle in the sky,
    the way of a snake on a rock,
the way of a ship on the high seas,
    and the way of a man with a young woman.

²⁰ "This is the way of an adulterous woman:
    She eats and wipes her mouth
    and says, 'I've done nothing wrong.'

²¹ "Under three things the earth trembles,
    under four it cannot bear up:
²² a servant who becomes king,

a godless fool who gets plenty to eat,
²³ a contemptible woman who gets married,
    and a servant who displaces her mistress.

²⁴ "Four things on earth are small,
    yet they are extremely wise:
²⁵ Ants are creatures of little strength,
    yet they store up their food in the summer;
²⁶ hyraxes are creatures of little power,
    yet they make their home in the crags;
²⁷ locusts have no king,
    yet they advance together in ranks;
²⁸ a lizard can be caught with the hand,
    yet it is found in kings' palaces.

²⁹ "There are three things that are stately in their stride,
    four that move with stately bearing:
³⁰ a lion, mighty among beasts,
    who retreats before nothing;
³¹ a strutting rooster, a he-goat,
    and a king secure against revolt.

³² "If you play the fool and exalt yourself,
    or if you plan evil,
    clap your hand over your mouth!
³³ For as churning cream produces butter,
    and as twisting the nose produces blood,
    so stirring up anger produces strife."

Believing Truth

–XOCHITL DIXON

Every word of God is flawless;
he is a shield to those who take refuge in him.

PROVERBS 30:5

I set my Bible on the podium and stared at the eager faces waiting for me to begin the message. I'd prayed and prepared. Why couldn't I speak?

You're worthless. No one will ever listen to you, especially if they know your past. And God would never use you. Seared into my heart and mind, the words spoken in various ways over my life ignited a decade-long war against the lies I so easily believed. Though I knew the words weren't true, I couldn't seem to escape my insecurities and fears. So, I opened my Bible.

Turning to Proverbs 30:5, I inhaled and exhaled slowly before reading out loud. "Every word of God is flawless," I said, "he is a shield to those who take refuge in him." I closed my eyes as peace overwhelmed me, and I began to share my testimony with the crowd.

Many of us have experienced the paralyzing power of negative words or opinions others have of us. However, God's words are "flawless," perfect and absolutely sound. When we're tempted to believe spirit-crushing ideas about our value or our purpose as God's children, God's enduring and infallible truth protects our minds and our hearts. We can echo the psalmist who wrote: "I remember, LORD, your ancient laws, and I find comfort in them" (Psalm 119:52).

Let's combat lies we've accepted about God, ourselves, and others by replacing negative-speak with Scripture. 🕭

MEET AGUR SON OF JAKEH, KING LEMUEL, AND THE QUEEN MOTHER

In the final two chapters of Proverbs, we are introduced to two new authors: a sage, Agur (chapter 30), and a king named Lemuel (chapter 31). Though we know very little about them, they give us rich insights to wrap up our journey in Proverbs, including a call for humility before God in 30:2–4 that's reminiscent of Job 38–41, observations from the natural world (30:15–19, 24–30), and the celebration of a valiant woman (31:10–31).

Proverbs also concludes with the words of wisdom from another powerful woman—King Lemuel's mother, the queen mother, whose words are recorded by her son. She teaches Lemuel about leadership (vv. 1–9), advising him to unleash justice and to stand for the marginalized and oppressed (vv. 8–9).

WISDOM IN NATURE

insight

If you seek wisdom, go outside your front door! That's the message of the wise man Agur. In chapter 30, Agur tells us the natural world is our classroom for practical knowledge. So, to discover wisdom . . . watch an eagle fly (v. 19). Catch a lizard in your hand (v. 28). Observe locusts marching in file (v. 27). They will tell you the order of things—and reveal the brilliance of our kind, wise Creator.

What lies about God, yourself, or others have you believed?

What verses in the Bible have helped you see God, yourself, and others through the truth of Scripture?

Proverbs 31

¹ *The sayings of King Lemuel—*

an inspired utterance his mother taught him.

² Listen, my son! Listen, son of my womb!
Listen, my son, the answer to my prayers!
³ Do not spend your strength on women,
your vigor on those who ruin kings.

⁴ It is not for kings, Lemuel—
it is not for kings to drink wine,
not for rulers to crave beer,
⁵ lest they drink and forget what has been decreed,
and deprive all the oppressed of their rights.
⁶ Let beer be for those who are perishing,
wine for those who are in anguish!
⁷ Let them drink and forget their poverty
and remember their misery no more.

⁸ Speak up for those who cannot speak for themselves,
for the rights of all who are destitute.
⁹ Speak up and judge fairly;
defend the rights of the poor and needy.